FROM AARON TO ZERUBBABEL

FROM AARON TO ZERUBBABEL

Profiles of Bible People

Iris V. Cully
and
Kendig Brubaker Cully

HAWTHORN BOOKS, INC.
Publishers-New York

Introduction

This book is designed to enable a teacher or other student of the Bible to find quickly the most important facts about persons who figure in the biblical accounts. All important characters are included, as well as many who did not play such key roles as to get any detailed attention in the records. It is hoped that these brief biographical sketches will be useful for those who come across characters in the Bible toward whom they would like to have a brief orientation before delving into more detailed study. Others will find these sketches a convenient way to refresh their memory about characters whom they know in general but forget specifically. Teachers and parents will find story material.

Nowhere in the Bible do we find a complete biography of any character. Biography in the modern sense of a "complete life story" was not the concern of the biblical writers. Yet personalities are mainly the key factor in historical events (as well as in story material); hence many persons are referred to, in greater or less detail. In the Judeo-Christian tradition, these biblical characters for centuries have been the instruments through whom the people of faith have been introduced to the ways of God with man, and man with God. They can come alive in our experience when we become familiar with such facts about them as are available.

Those who wish more detailed information will want to consult reference books such as *Dictionary of the Bible*, edited by John L. McKenzie, S.J. (The Bruce Publishing Company, 1965); *The Interpreter's Dictionary of the Bible* (4 vols.), edited by George A. Buttrick, *et al.* (Abingdon Press, 1962); *The Westminster Dictionary of the Bible*, edited by J. D. Davis and H. S. Gehman (The Westminster Press, 1959).

Quotations from the Bible are taken from the Revised Standard Version of the Bible, copyrighted 1946 and 1952 by the Division of Christian Education, National Council of the Churches of Christ in the U.S.A., and are used by permission.

The pronunciation of names is offered, by permission, from the Self-pronouncing Edition, *The Holy Bible*, published by The World Publishing Company.

Key to Pronunciation

The pronunciation marking system listed below will enable the student and teacher to easily read and pronounce the names of the men and women listed in this Bible study guide. Each name is separated into syllables, and an accent mark (′) is placed after the syllable to receive the main stress. Where names are already well-known (such as Adam, John, Ruth, Saul), no pronunciation marks are given.

a	*as in*	cat	ȯ	*as in*	comply
ā	" "	cāke	u	" "	up
ä	" "	cär	ū	" "	ūse
ȧ	" "	ȧbout	ü	" "	rüle
â	" "	câre	u̇	" "	focu̇s
e	" "	ten	ūr	" "	fūrther
ē	" "	ēven	y	" "	happy
ė	" "	agėnt or fathėr			
ēr	" "	hērd	ȳ	" "	lȳre
i	" "	it or sanity	äi	= i	*as in* äisle
ī	" "	bīte	ch	= k	" " ache
ĭ	" "	bĭrd	ċ	= s	" " ċite
o	" "	lot	ġ	= j	" " ġem
ō	" "	gō	ṡ	= z	" " thoṡe
ô	" "	hôrn	ẋ	= z	" " ẋylophone

All other consonents are pronounced with their usual sounds in English, as ph = f, c = k, etc.

FROM AARON TO ZERUBBABEL

Aaron Aâ'ron

Aaron was the brother of Moses and Miriam. When Moses was called to present to Pharaoh a request for permission for the people of Israel to leave Egypt and to go into the desert to sacrifice to their God, Aaron was appointed to speak in place of the inarticulate Moses. He was often close to Moses during the wilderness journey. One day while a battle was taking place, Aaron and Hur held up Moses' hands for many hours. Moses left Aaron in charge of the people during the ascent to Mount Sinai. It was during Moses' absence that Aaron permitted the people to make a golden calf to worship. He was not punished as were the others, because he had done this in response to their plea.

Aaron was appointed high priest and his sons were appointed priests to serve under him. Their priesthood was reaffirmed by the judgment which ended the rebellion of the family of Korah, who were Levites. Aaron died before entering the Promised Land, and the office of high priest was given to his son Eleazar. (Exod. 4; 7; 24; 32; Lev. 8; Num. 16; 20)

Abednego A·bed'ne·gō

One of a group of young princes from Judah, exiled to Babylon, who were chosen for three years of special training in the service of King Nebuchadnezzar. Daniel, their leader, secured permission for himself, Abednego, Shadrach, and Meshach to eat simple food, in keeping with the Jewish dietary laws, instead of the rich diet prescribed for them. At the end of their training period, these four surpassed all others in their development, and were appointed to govern the province of Babylon. Later, refusing to worship a golden image of the king, the four young men were put into a burning furnace. To the astonishment of all, they moved about unharmed, and the king ordered their release. They had convinced him of the power of their God. (Daniel)

Abel Ā′bel

Abel, the second son of Adam and Eve, was a shepherd. He offered to God a sacrifice of lambs, and this offering was accepted. One day his older brother Cain, a farmer, jealous because God had not accepted a grain offering, asked Abel to go into a field with him. There Cain murdered Abel. (Gen. 4)

Abiathar Á·bī′á·thär

King Saul, fearing the power of young David, learned from a spy that one of the priestly families had visited David. He ordered their deaths, and only Abiathar escaped. Abiathar went to David, taking with him the sacred ephod, through which he sought the will of God in the king's behalf. When David became king, he became a trusted adviser, serving as a member of the king's council. During the revolt of the king's son Absalom, Abiathar was responsible for moving the ark from the troubled city of Jerusalem. Later, he was asked to return with it, and while back in the capital he acted as a spy to get messages into the hands of the king, who had fled. In his old age he favored Adonijah, the king's oldest son, as David's successor. Instead, Solomon won the struggle for the kingship, and Abiathar fled to the tabernacle for refuge. King Solomon spared his life, but removed him from his priesthood and retired him to his home. (I Sam. 22:9; 23:6; I Chron. 15:11; 27:34; II Sam. 15; I Kings 1, 2)

Abigail Ab′i·gāil

Abigail was the wife of Nabal, a rich man of Carmel. When David was in exile as an outlaw from Saul, he had protected Nabal's land and cattle. One day David sent messengers to Nabal to ask for food and was refused. David prepared to take supplies by force. Some of Nabal's servants, hearing of this, told Abigail what was happening. Abigail immediately gathered supplies, sought out David, and begged him to accept the gifts and spare the household. Accepting her gifts, David praised her wisdom. When Abigail returned to the house, Nabal was feasting. The account of what she had done disturbed him greatly. Ten days later Nabal died, and David married Abigail. On one occasion during a raid by the Amalekites, she was captured but was rescued by David and his men. She accompanied him to Hebron when he was crowned king of Judah. She bore him one son. (I Sam. 25; 27; 30; II Sam. 2)

Abijah   À·bī′jàh

Abijah (also called Abijam), son of Rehoboam, was king of Judah, 915–913 B.C. He is criticized in I Kings, probably for permitting the worship of idols and not being himself completely faithful to God. During a war with Jeroboam, king of Israel, although surrounded by enemy troops, he won the battle and pursued Jeroboam, capturing several villages. (I Kings 15; II Chron. 13)

Abijam   À·bī′jàm *(see* **Abijah***)*

Abimelech   À·bim′è·lech

(1) Abimelech, one of the sons of Gideon, made himself ruler in Israel by murdering his many brothers and persuading the rest of the tribe to accept him as their leader. Three years later the people of Shechem revolted, but Abimelech was able to put down the uprising. He carried the battle to Thebez, where the people fled to a fortified tower. When Abimelech tried to burn it, a woman released a millstone, which hit him on the head. The wounded Abimelech called his armor-bearer to complete his death with a sword, lest it be said that a woman killed him. Like the other judges, he was chiefly a military leader who both defended the land held by the Israelites and, whenever possible, extended it. (Judg. 8:29–9:1–57)

(2) Abimelech was a Canaanite king, who, not knowing that Sarah was the wife of Abraham, took her into his harem, but hastily released her when he discovered his

mistake. Abimelech made a treaty with Abraham, guaranteeing him rights to a well he had dug and to pasture-land in the Negeb. (Gen. 20)

Abiram   À·bī′ràm *(see* **Moses***)*

Abishag   Ab′i·shag *(see* **Adonijah***)*

Abishai   À·bī′shäi

Abishai was one of David's closest associates throughout his life. When the outlawed young leader slipped past the guard into the presence of the sleeping King Saul, Abishai, who was with him, urged David to kill the king, but David refused. Later Abishai was involved in the murder of Abner, military leader in the household of Saul, who had come to David and had been granted pardon. This was done to avenge the earlier killing of Abishai's brother by Abner. Abishai commanded part of the army of David under his brother Joab. During the revolt of David's son Absalom, Abishai remained faithful to the king. He is mentioned in the list of David's heroes, having spent his whole lifetime in both personal and official service, being loyal to the king above all others. (I Sam. 26; II Sam. 2–3; 10; 16–18; 21; 23:18–19)

Abner   Ăb′nēr

Abner was Saul's cousin and commander of his army. He introduced young David to the king at the battle with the Philistines. His high rank in David's household is indicated by the fact that he dined at the king's table. He was guarding Saul at the time David successfully entered the camp but left without killing the king. After Saul's army had been defeated in battle and three of the king's sons had been killed, Abner fled with Ishbaal, Saul's remaining son, who reigned over Israel. David became king of Judah. When war broke out between the two kingdoms, Abner's men were defeated in a tournament at the pool of Gibeon. Pursued, he killed Asahel, brother of Joab and Abishai, David's commanders. Abner's loyalty to Saul's family ended when the king accused him of taking a woman from Saul's harem. Deciding that David alone could bring peace and unite the people, he urged the tribes of Israel to accept David as their king. Then he met with David and promised to try to bring about this covenant. David accepted the offer. When Joab heard of this he sent for Abner, who came unsuspectingly and was murdered to avenge Asahel's killing. Lamenting his death, David said, "A prince and a great man has fallen this day in Israel." But the death was helpful to him, weakening Ish-bosheth's now leaderless army, and Joab went unpunished. (I Sam. 17; 20; 26; II Sam. 2–3)

Abraham Ā′brȧ·hȧm

The original name of Abraham was Abram. He was born in the Chaldean city Ur. During his young manhood he and his wife Sarah, as part of the household of his father, Terah, emigrated to Haran. After Terah's death he became head of the family and heard God's call to go into the land of the Canaanites. Across the years he pitched his tent in many places, each time building an altar to the Lord. When a long drought produced famine, he went into Egypt to buy food. However, many favorable seasons permitted his cattle to increase, and he became wealthy. For the most part he was able to live in peace with the native inhabitants, but sometimes there were quarrels with tribal chieftains. Tension arose between the herdsmen of Abraham and those of his nephew, Lot, who grew restless and obtained Abraham's permission to resettle in the fertile Jordan River valley. Later, Abraham rescued Lot, first from abducting chieftains and then from burning Sodom.

Abraham's first son, Ishmael, was the child of his concubine, Hagar. However, it was not Ishmael but another son, Isaac, who was the heir through whom the line of Israel was to develop. For God, in calling Abraham to this wandering life in Canaan, had promised to pass on the land to Abraham's descendants. When Abraham was ninety-nine years old, God made a covenant with him, and his family: God would be their God forever, and they would be his people. They would increase throughout the generations, inheriting this land. He would bless them, and through them all nations would be blessed. He required of them faithfulness and obedience. The sign of the covenant was to be the circumcision of all male infants. It was at this time that Abram's name became Abraham, which means "exalted father."

When Isaac was still young, God tested Abraham by requiring him to take the boy to a distant place and offer him as a sacrifice. At the last minute the father's hand was stayed, and he was commended for his obedience. Abraham, remembering the promise, had trusted that God would fulfill his word. He lived to see Isaac married to a cousin, Rebekah. At an advanced age he died, still confident that God would continue to bless his family, and was buried in a lot he had purchased at Hebron, beside Sarah, his wife. (Gen. 11:31–25:11)

Absalom   Ab'sà·lòm

Absalom, son of David, was second in succession to the throne. When his half-brother Amnon raped his sister Tamar, Absalom planned revenge for two years. Then he invited Amnon to a sheep-shearing festival, during which he murdered Amnon. He fled and stayed away for three years, after which the king decided that murder within a family should not be avenged. Returning, Absalom was not admitted to the king's presence for two more years. He became popular among the people for his handsomeness and charm, and he encouraged them to look upon him as one who would provide justice of the sort the king had evidently neglected. Four years later he gathered a following at Hebron and declared himself king. David fled from Jerusalem to the Mount of Olives, while Absalom entered the city and took possession of the king's harem, an act of treason. Absalom's counselor urged immediate battle, but the prince followed the counsel of Hushai, who suggested delay while an army was gathered which Absalom would personally lead. Unknown to all, Hushai was David's secret agent, who relayed this information to the king. The delay benefited David. Finally the two forces met in battle at Ephraim. Absalom's men were routed and he fled on a mule. But his long hair, of which he was proud, caught in the branches of a tree. Joab, the king's commander, found and killed him, despite the king's orders to spare his son. David lamented the death of his worthless son until Joab rebuked him, saying that he should, rather, rejoice in the loyalty of those who had saved the kingdom and the king. (II Sam. 13–19)

Achan Ā′chăn

En route to the Promised Land, the Israelites attacked the city of Jericho. They had been ordered to take no booty, for all was to be devoted to God and burned. However, Achan of the tribe of Judah disobeyed. This was discovered when a defeat at Ai disclosed the displeasure of the Lord. Through a process of sifting each tribe and each family by lot, Achan was discovered, and he then confessed. In punishment he, his family, his possessions, and the stolen goods were removed to the valley of Achor. There the people were stoned and burned and buried along with their goods. The sin was thus removed from Israel. (Josh. 7)

Adam Ad′am

The word "adam" in Hebrew means "man," and has been capitalized as the name for the first man. His creation by the word of God on the sixth day was the climax of creation. He was set in a garden where provision was made for all his needs. He was given authority over all other living creatures, symbolized by his naming each one. A woman was given to him for his companion. His body was formed from the earth, and God breathed life into him. One thing was forbidden: he must not eat from the tree of the knowledge of good and evil. But Adam, yielding to his wife who had been tempted by Satan, ate this fruit. Ashamed of himself and his wife, he made them clothes and hid from God. God discovered him and confronted him with his disobedience. For punishment he was expelled from the garden and told that henceforth work would be heavy, that the ground would not yield food easily, and that finally he would die. Adam was the father of three sons: Cain, Abel, and Seth. (Gen. 1–4)

Adonijah Ad·ò·nī′jàh

Adonijah was the oldest surviving son of David in the king's old age. Supported by both Joab and Abiathar, life-long counselors of David's, he felt assured that he would become king. He gave a banquet for his supporters to celebrate his hope. Nathan, who supported Solomon, heard of this and warned Bathsheba, knowing that a new king would destroy remaining contenders. She persuaded David to appoint her son Solomon to share the kingdom, and at David's command Solomon was anointed to become his successor as ruler. The news of this arrived during Adonijah's party, and he fled to the altar for safety. Solomon spared his life, ordering him to remain in his own house.

After King David's death, Adonijah made one other play for power. He asked Bathsheba to inquire of King Solomon whether he might marry Abishag, the young girl who had served the king in his last illness. Since marrying a member of the royal harem was itself a sign of royal power, Solomon interpreted the request as an indication that Adonijah still had hopes of gaining influence, and ordered Adonijah's death. (I Kings 1; 2:13–25)

Agabus Ag'à·bùs

Agabus was one of the prophets in the early church. Sent from Jerusalem to Antioch on a mission, he stood up in a meeting of the Christian community and declared that there would be a widespread famine. This occurred during the reign of Emperor Claudius (A.D. 49). The church at Antioch responded by sending relief to their brethren in Jerusalem. Years later, when the apostle Paul was visiting Caesarea on the way to Jerusalem, Agabus sought him. To dramatize his words he took Paul's girdle and bound his own hands and feet, announcing that the Holy Spirit said Paul would be bound and delivered to the Gentiles if he went to Jerusalem. Although Paul was not dissuaded from proceeding, Agabus' words proved correct. (Acts 11:27–30; 21:10–15)

Agrippa À·grip'pà

Marcus Julius Agrippa (Agrippa II) succeeded to his father's kingdom in A.D. 50 while he was still very young. (An uncle had been regent for eight years.) Three years later his territories were extended to include parts of Galilee and Perea. He carefully cultivated the good will of the Jews by respecting their laws and customs. Agrippa is mentioned in the New Testament because he was present in Caesarea when the new procurator, Festus, was hearing charges against the apostle Paul. Festus discussed the situation with King Agrippa, who asked to hear Paul. This hearing was the occasion for a presentation of the apostolic preaching of the gospel. Agrippa responded by saying that Paul almost had persuaded him to be a Christian. It was Agrippa's opinion that Paul should be released, but Paul had already appealed to Caesar, and nothing could override that petition. (Acts 25–26)

Ahab Ā'hab

Ahab, the seventh king of Israel (859–854 B.C.), is notorious in the biblical record for condoning the cult of Baal, introduced from Tyre by his wife, Jezebel. This cult was challenged by the prophet Elijah in the competing sacrifices on Mount Carmel, to the discomfiture of the priests of Baal and the vindication of the God of Israel. At a later time, when Israel was threatened by the king of Samaria, Ahab, on the advice of a prophet, went into battle and repulsed him on two separate occasions. After the surrender he spared the king's life, and thereby incurred the wrath of a prophet who insisted that the invader should be killed. Ahab met Elijah again when the king sought to buy from one of his subjects land adjoining the palace. The man, Naboth, refused to sell his inheritance. Jezebel, by means of false letters, had Naboth accused of blasphemy and executed. Then Ahab confiscated the land for his own use. The prophet Elijah confronted the king with the injustice he had permitted, and cursed him, but the king repented and was forgiven. Ahab seems to have been a strong ruler who extended the boundaries of his kingdom and brought prosperity. Finally, after three years of war with Samaria, he was joined by the king of Judah in an effort to recover Ramoth-gilead. Prophets were consulted, and while many gave assurances of victory, one predicted defeat. During the battle, Ahab disguised himself but was struck by a chance arrow. Hoping to hold his troops together, he had himself propped up in his chariot, and stayed in the field all day, finally dying from loss of blood. The battle was lost. (I Kings 16:29–22:40)

Ahasuerus   À·has̆'ū·ē·rús

Ahasuerus was king of Persia 485–465 B.C., during the time when the people of Judah were exiled there. His armies fought against Greece but were defeated and he was assassinated. The book of Esther relates how he was angered by the refusal of his queen, Vashti, to appear before the people at a feast. He dismissed her and chose another favorite from his harem, Esther, a Jewish girl. When a plot to destroy the Jews was uncovered, Esther appeared before the king unbidden. He showed his favor toward her by listening to her story and encouraging a counterplot which led to the downfall of Haman, the court officer involved. (Esther)

Ahaz Ā'haz

Ahaz was king of Judah 735–715 B.C. Early in his reign the kings of Israel and Damascus urged him to join them against an invasion of the Assyrians. He refused, and when they turned against him, he appealed to Tiglath-pileser III of Assyria and became his vassal. The prophet Isaiah opposed this policy, counseling him to stay unallied and to trust in God. He warned that the alliance would be disastrous. In spite of the tribute paid to Assyria for protection, Ahaz had to face other invasions, from the Philistines and the Edomites. Ahaz made religious innovations, patterned after Assyria, including setting up of new altar and removing some of the furniture from the temple. This faithlessness to the God of Israel brought criticism from the prophet and from the writer of the Chronicles. (II Chron. 28; II Kings 16; Isa. 7)

Ahaziah Ā·hà·zī'àh

Ahaziah, the son of Ahab, was king of Israel for little more than one year (850–849 B.C.). He was involved with the king of Judah in an unsuccessful expedition against Ophir to obtain gold. One day he fell from a window. Helpless, he sent messengers for an oracle from Baalzebub, god of Ekron, concerning his recovery. The prophet Elijah, meeting them, turned them back, asking why the king could not inquire of the God of Israel. Elijah threatened him with death because of this faithlessness, and indeed the king did not recover. (I Kings 22:51–53; II Kings 1; 8:25–29)

Ahijah A·hī′jàh

Ahijah was a prophet at the time when the united kingdom of Israel was coming to an end. Sharing the dissatisfaction of many over King Solomon's idolatry and his oppression, Ahijah accosted an able young leader, Jeroboam. Removing his new cloak, he tore it into twelve pieces, giving ten to Jeroboam. This was to indicate that the sins of Solomon would result in the division of the kingdom, two tribes remaining under the house of David because of David's own faithfulness.

One time after Jeroboam became king of Judah, his son became ill, and the queen in disguise sought Ahijah for advice. Recognizing her, the prophet said that her son would die, but that this was a blessing, because most of the family in generations to come would die violently. Ahijah had become disappointed in the king, who seemed to be as idolatrous as his predecessor. (I Kings 11:29ff.; 14:1ff.)

Amasa À·mā′sà

Amasa, a nephew of King David, was loyal to Absalom in his rebellion, and the prince made him commander of his army. After the rebellion was put down, Amasa persuaded the men to reaffirm their allegiance to David. The king placed him in command of the army (replacing Joab, who had killed Absalom) and indicated his trust by sending Amasa to quell the revolt of Sheba ben Bichri. Joab, greeting him as he arrived to join the battle, killed him with one blow from the sword. (II Sam. 17:25; 19:14; 20:4ff.)

Amaziah Am·à·zī'àh

Amaziah was king of Judah 800–783 B.C. Showing mercy unusual in his time, he punished those who had murdered his father, King Joash, but spared their families, thereby respecting the Law (Deut. 24:16). He conducted a successful campaign against Edom, but when he challenged the king of Israel he was defeated and captured, the walls of Jerusalem were breached, and treasure was taken from the temple and the palace. Finally, a conspiracy forced him to flee to Lachish, where he was assassinated. The Chronicler describes him as one of the kings who did right in the sight of God, although he, like his father, permitted the people to worship elsewhere than in Jerusalem. (II Kings 14:1–22)

Amon Ā'mon *(see* **Manasseh***)*

Amos Ā'mos

The prophet Amos lived during the reign of Jeroboam II of Israel, and the words contained in the book bearing his name were probably spoken between 760 and 750 B.C. That was a time of peace and prosperity, a fact suggested by his descriptions of great houses and gardens, beds of ivory, feasts, and singing. Amos referred to himself as a shepherd from Tekoa, in Judah, and a dresser of sycamore trees. He insisted that he was not a professional prophet but that he spoke only because he could not deny the call of God upon him.

The prophet's forum was the shrine at Bethel, the capital of Israel, just over the border from Judah. His book opens dramatically with a series of judgments pronounced against the neighboring nations, each one coming closer home, until finally he announces God's judgment on Judah and then on Israel. In his continuing protests before the people of Israel, Amos pointed out that they were under special responsibility because they were God's chosen people. Their worship of sacrifices and tithes would not fulfill God's demands, since God is righteous and only a righteous people will satisfy him. Instead they trampled upon the needy, selling the poor for small debts. They took bribes. They gave short weight when they sold grain.

Finally, the priest Amaziah ordered Amos to leave Bethel, the king's sanctuary, and preach judgment to his own country, Judah. This only evoked further protest from the prophet, who insisted that his words were true because they were spoken at the call of God. Israel, he said, would be destroyed, and its people scattered, because they paid only lip-service to God and refused to keep his righteous Law. (Amos)

Ananias   An·à·nī′às

(1) Ananias and his wife, Sapphira, were members of the early Christian community in Jerusalem. When the Christians pooled all their resources, Ananias sold a piece of land but, in agreement with his wife, withheld part of the proceeds. He brought the remainder to Peter as if it were the whole, but the apostle detected the deception.

Peter insisted that since no one was forcing Ananias either to sell the land or to give the proceeds to the community, his deliberate deception was a lie to God. Shocked, Ananias fell dead at Peter's feet. A few hours later, his unsuspecting wife arrived, repeated the deceit in answer to Peter's questioning, was told of her husband's death, and likewise fell dead. (Acts 5:1ff.)

(2) Ananias was a Jewish Christian living in Damascus, to whom the word of the Lord came, telling him to seek out Saul. Ananias protested that Saul meant only to do evil to the church, but he was assured that Saul had been chosen by God for a special work. So Ananias went to the house of one Judas on Straight Street. Entering, he greeted Saul as brother, laid his hands on his eyes, bade him regain his sight and receive the gift of the Holy Spirit. He told Saul that he was to be a witness and urged him to be baptized immediately. (Acts 9:10ff; 22:12-16)

Andrew   Ản'drew

Andrew was one of the twelve disciples of Jesus. He was the brother of Peter and a follower of John the Baptist. When John affirmed that Jesus was the Lamb of God, Andrew visited Jesus and became his disciple. While he and Peter were fishing on the Sea of Galilee one day, Jesus saw them and called them to become fishers of men. The two left their boat and remained with him from that time. Andrew sensed the needs of people who sought Jesus. When the crowd had gathered to see Jesus and there was no food, Andrew was the one who pointed out the boy with the loaves and fish. At Passover time, when some Greeks asked the disciples if they could see Jesus, Andrew carried the request to their Master. He is not mentioned in the book of Acts, so it is not known what work he carried out in the early days of the church. (Mark 1:16ff.; John 1:40–44; 6:8; 12:22)

Anna Àn'nà

Anna was a prophetess in Jerusalem in Jesus' time. She became widowed while still young and lived to be eighty-four years old. She was a devout woman who fasted often and constantly worshiped in the temple. When Mary and Joseph brought the infant Jesus to the temple at the time of Mary's purification (according to custom, forty days after his birth), she came to them, giving thanks to God and hailing this child as the promised redeemer. (Luke 2:36)

Annas An'nàs

Annas was appointed high priest in A.D. 6 but was deposed nine years later. In the succeeding years the office was held by five of his sons and by Caiaphas, his son-in-law, with whom his name is mentioned in connection with the trial of Jesus. There they interrogate the prisoner even before Jesus appears before the Sanhedrin. When the apostles began their preaching, Peter and John were arrested and later brought before Annas and others from the priestly family to make their defense. (John 18:13ff.; Acts 4:6ff.)

Antipas   An'ti·pàs *(see* **Herod Antipas***)*

Apollos   À·pol'los

Apollos was a Jew, a native of Alexandria, an important city in the first-century Roman empire. He was an eloquent speaker, well-educated in the scriptures, and a follower of John the Baptist. He had been instructed in the way of Jesus and he taught fervently and accurately according to his knowledge. Apollos moved to Ephesus and began to preach in the synagogue there. He met Priscilla and Aquila who, after hearing him, began to teach him about Jesus as they had learned from Paul. Encouraged by the church at Ephesus, he traveled to Corinth, spoke with the people there, and preached to the Jews that Jesus was the Messiah. Paul wrote of him as a co-worker, but when the parties surrounding Apollos and other leaders in the Corinthian church grew too strong, the apostle broke them up. Paul, writing much later to Titus at Crete, asked him to encourage Apollos on his journey; thus it can be surmised that this forceful preacher continued his work and witness. (Acts 18:24ff., I Cor. 1:10ff., Tit. 3:13)

Aquila   Aq'ui·là

Aquila was a Jew from Pontus, a city of the Roman empire. He and his wife, Priscilla, had lived in Rome but when the emperor Claudius expelled the Jews from the imperial city they moved to Corinth. There Paul met them, and lived with them while in the city because he shared

Aquila's trade of tentmaker. They were probably among his first converts in that city. When he moved to Ephesus, they accompanied him. Zealous for the faith, they heard Apollos preach, instructed him more fully, and saw him begin his work as a witness to Jesus the Messiah. They must have lived in Ephesus for many years, because Paul sent greetings to them in several of his letters. At some time, however, they returned to live in Rome, and when Paul wrote to the church there he expressed gratitude because they had once risked their lives to save him. (Acts 18:1–4, 18–19, 24ff.; Rom. 16:3)

Artaxerxes   Är·tá·xêrx'ēs̱

Artaxerxes was the reigning Persian king during the time of Ezra and Nehemiah when the Jews were being permitted to return to Jerusalem to rebuild the walls and the temple. Nehemiah was butler to Artexerxes, and his nearness to the king may have provided the influence by which his desire to return and rebuild was granted. It is difficult to establish the chronology, but it is thought that Artexerxes I gave Nehemiah the authority to rebuild the walls of Jerusalem and that Artaxerxes II was the king in whose reign the exiles under Ezra were permitted to return to rebuild the temple. (Neh. 2:1ff.; Ezra 7:1ff.)

Asa   Ā'sà

Asa, king of Judah (913–873 B.C.), was considered a good king. He removed the idols from the temple and discouraged foreign cults, even deposing his mother from her position as queen mother because she practiced one of these cults. He gathered the people together to renew their covenant with God. He gave gifts of gold and silver to the temple. In these reforms, he had the counsel of the prophet Azariah. The land was prosperous and at peace for many years, and Asa felt assured that this was God's favor shown to Israel because of their faithfulness. Once he repelled an invasion from the Ethiopians. At another time he fought off an invasion from Israel by paying the king of Damascus to attack Israel. The money came both from the temple treasure and from the palace treasury, and the whole endeavor was condemned by the prophet Hanani. The prophets always insisted that kings should trust in God rather than in alliances with other kings. Asa was so angry that he imprisoned the prophet and punished some of the other people involved. Late in life Asa suffered a disease in his feet and sought help from doctors, but not, says the Chronicler, from the Lord. He died in the forty-first year of his reign and was buried with honor. (I Kings 15:9-24; II Chron. 14-16)

Asahel   As'à·hel *(see* **Abner***)*

Athaliah   Ath·à·lī'àh

Athaliah was the daughter of Ahab and Jezebel of Israel and was married to Jehoram, king of Judah, an evil king who ruled for eight years. Her son, Ahaziah, was no better. He was killed by Jehu in a revolt. Athaliah then assassinated the royal family and reigned as queen in

Judah for six years. But Joash, an infant son of Ahaziah, had been saved by his sister and hidden in the temple where he was brought up by the priest Johoiada. After winning the loyalty of the palace guard, Jehoiada proclaimed the young child king. Athaliah, going to investigate the event, was captured and slain. (II Kings 8:18, 26; 11:1ff.)

Augustus Au·gùs'tùs

Augustus was the Roman emperor at the time of the birth of Jesus. Nephew and adopted son of Julius Caesar, he ascended the throne upon the latter's death and reigned from 31 B.C. to A.D. 13. His name was Gaius Octavianus; the term "Augustus" is a title meaning "the venerable." He was a patron of Herod the Great and confirmed him as king of the Jews. (Luke 2:1)

Azariah Az·à·rī'àh *(see* **Abednego; Uzziah***)***

Baasha Bā'à·shà

Baasha belonged to the tribe of Issachar in the kingdom of Israel. He was a soldier in the army of King Nadab, son of Jeroboam I, while it was laying siege to one of the cities of the Philistines. He started a conspiracy against the king and assassinated him. After proclaiming himself ruler of Israel, he ordered the death of everyone belonging to the house of Jeroboam, seeking thereby to prevent other claimants to the throne. He immediately declared war on Judah (where Asa was king) by fortifying the border city of Ramah, seeking thus to prevent entrance to Jerusalem. His plan was thwarted when Asa paid the king of Damascus to divert the army of Baasha. So Baasha stopped the building operation and made Tirzah his capital. He continued to carry on war against Judah throughout his reign. Despite warnings of judgment from a prophet, he continued his evil ways through a twenty-four-year reign. (I Kings 15:16-22, 33-16:7)

Balaam Bā'laam

Balaam was a seer or prophet at Pethor who lived at the time the Hebrews were entering the Promised Land. The king of Moab, alarmed by the approach of a people who, he was sure, would overwhelm his country, sent high officials bearing gifts, requesting the prophet to curse the invaders. Balaam, warned by God, refused to do so. A second time the officials came, and this time God told Balaam to accompany them to the king but to do only what the Lord should tell him. As they traveled along the road, three times the ass on which Balaam rode balked and Balaam struck it. Finally the animal spoke, protesting its faithfulness, and Balaam saw an angel standing in the way. Again he was warned to speak only as he was told. Elaborate sacrifices were offered and then Balaam began to speak. To the dismay of King Balak, four times the prophet blessed Israel, and disclosed its eventual victory over Moab. Then Balaam returned to Pethor. (Num. 22-24)

Balak   Bā′lȧk

Balak was the king of Moab who consulted the prophet Balaam at the approach of the Israelites. (*See* **Balaam**)

Barabbas   Bȧ·rab′bȧs

Barabbas was a Zealot, one of those revolutionaries in first-century Judea who refused to submit to the rule of Rome and who tried to foment revolt. Such men lived dangerously and some among them were also known to be bandits and murderers. Barabbas (the name means "son of the father") was in prison when Jesus was brought to trial. It was customary to release a prisoner in honor of Passover and Pilate gave the assembled people a choice between Jesus and Barabbas. They called for Barabbas and, in a literal sense, Jesus died in his place. (Mark 15:7ff.)

Barak   Bâr′ȧk

When the Israelites were settling in the land of Canaan, they were at one time under the oppressive rule of a Canaanite king. Deborah became a judge in Israel and summoned Barak to raise an army from among the tribes and go into battle against Sisera, commander of the king's troops. Inspired by the presence of Deborah with the army, Barak defeated Sisera at Mount Tabor and the Israelites were freed. (Jud. 4–5)

Bar-Jesus   Bär-Jē′süs *(see* **Sergius Paulus***)*

Barnabas Bär-nà·bàs

Joseph Barnabas, a Jew of a priestly family (Levite), was born in Cyprus. He belonged to the earliest Christian community in Jerusalem and was among the first to sell his land and give the proceeds for distribution to the poor. When Saul (Paul), who had left Jerusalem breathing threats against the church, returned announcing that he had become a Christian, the church was afraid to believe him. Barnabas alone received him, took him to the apostles, and recounted the story of his conversion.

When the Christians at Jerusalem, most of whom were of Jewish background, heard that Christians at Antioch were preaching to Greeks, they sent Barnabas, because of his own Cypriote background, to investigate. He was so encouraged by the growth of the church there that he went to Tarsus and brought Paul back to help him. They worked together for a year and then went to Jerusalem bearing a relief offering to the Christians at a time of famine. After their return to Antioch, they were selected by the elders to preach the gospel in new places. Taking with them Barnabas' cousin, John Mark, they traveled to Cyprus, Perga, Pisidian Antioch and the city of Lycaonia. At Lystra they were acclaimed as gods, and when they protested were stoned out of the city.

After the return to Antioch, the controversy over the observance of Jewish rites by Gentile converts arose, and Barnabas, with Paul, went to the council being held at Jerusalem. At first, according to Paul, Barnabas, like Peter, refused to eat with the Gentiles, but at the council he agreed with Paul that Gentile converts should not be required to observe Jewish rites. Upon their return to Antioch, Barnabas suggested that Mark go with them again on a preaching trip, but since the young man had left the earlier mission midway, Paul refused. The two separated. Barnabas and Mark returned to Cyprus. Although Barnabas and Paul did not travel together again, the breach must have been healed, for Barnabas is commended in the letter to the Corinthians. (Acts 4:36; 9:27; 11:22–26; 13–15; 29–30; Gal. 2:13; I Cor. 9:6)

Bartholomew   Bär·thŏl'ŏ·mew

Bartholomew, son of Tolmai, is simply listed as one of the twelve disciples. He has sometimes been identified with Nathanael, who is mentioned in John's Gospel as a fellow townsman of Philip from Bethsaida who was brought by Philip to see Jesus. Matt. 10:3; Mark 3:18; Luke 6:14; John 1:45; Acts 1:13)

Bartimaeus   Bär·ti·maē'ŭs

Bartimaeus, whose name means "son of Timaeus," was the blind beggar of Jericho whose persistent faith brought the healing word from Jesus. The Gospel writer contrasts this faith with the blindness of the disciples, who did not recognize who their master really was. (Mark 10:46–52; Luke 18:35–43)

Baruch   Bâr'ŭch

Baruch was the friend and secretary of the prophet Jeremiah. In the year 605 B.C. the prophet dictated to him a scroll containing a complete record of the words he had spoken to the people up to that time, warning of the fall of Jerusalem. Baruch read the words to the people assembled in the temple on a fast day. Upon invitation, he read them again to the officers of King Jehoiakim. Concerned about the criticism it implied of the king, they advised him to flee with Jeremiah and go into hiding. The king called for a reading of the words and destroyed the scroll column by column as he heard it read. Jeremiah promptly dictated the scroll again, with additions. During the siege of Jerusalem, when Jeremiah, by buying property, demonstrated his faith that God would eventually restore his people, the deed was put into Baruch's keeping. When Baruch complained of the bitterness of life, Jeremiah assured him that he (Baruch) would survive those troublous times. Those who remained in Jerusalem after the fall of the city wished to flee, but Jeremiah rebuked them. Baruch was blamed for encouraging the prophet to give this counsel. Both were forcibly taken to Egypt with those who fled there. (Jer. 32:11ff.; 36; 45)

Bathsheba Bath·she′bá

Bathsheba was the wife of Uriah, a Hittite and an officer in King David's army. She was seen by the king one day as she was bathing on the roof of her house. He called her to the palace and seduced her. The king, learning later that she had become pregnant and hoping to conceal the seduction, called Uriah home, but he refused to sleep in his own house while his fellow soldiers were in the battlefield. David's solution was to have Uriah put on the battle-

front to be killed. David subsequently married Bathsheba.
The child of their adultery died, but four other sons were
born to them. At Bathsheba's petition, David designated
her son Solomon to become his successor. Later she tried
diplomacy on her son when Adonijah, an unsuccessful
candidate for the throne, requested a young member of
David's harem for his own; but the request was refused.
(II Sam. 11:17ff.; 12:15ff.; I Kings 1:11–31; 2:12–23)

Belshazzar   Bel·shaz'zår

Belshazzar was the last ruler of Babylon and co-regent
for eight years with his father during the latter's absence
in Arabia. The book of Daniel relates how he gave a feast
in which the guests drank from goblets captured from the
temple at Jerusalem. Mysterious writing, suddenly appearing on the wall, caused terror. Daniel, called upon to
interpret the words, warned of the king's death and the
end of Babylonian power. That night Cyrus, king of Persia,
captured the city. (Dan. 5)

Belteshazzar   Bel·te·shaz'zår *(see* **Daniel***)*

Benaiah   Be·nā·'iàh

Benaiah was an officer of King David's and commander
of the king's bodyguard. He was one of David's thirty special men, and several of his deeds of personal courage are
recounted. He slew a lion on a snowy day, and he slew an
Egyptian by snatching the man's own sword. In David's
old age, Benaiah joined those who favored the candidacy
of Solomon as the king's successor. At the command of the

king, Benaiah with the royal guard escorted Solomon to his anointing. After the death of David, Benaiah, carrying out King Solomon's command, executed the rival claimant, Adonijah, who had fled to the altar for safety, and was appointed commander of the army in his place. (II Sam. 8:18; 23:20–23; I Kings 1:8,38; 2:23–25,43; 4:4)

Benjamin Ben'ja·min

Benjamin was the son of Jacob and the younger of the two sons of Rachel, who died soon after his birth. He was the only one of Jacob's sons to be born in Canaan and one of the twelve tribes is named for him. So careful was Jacob of this youngest son that when the others went to Egypt seeking grain, he was kept at home. Only at the insistence of Joseph, who was as yet unrecognized, and with solemn assurance for his safety by Judah, was he finally permitted to accompany them. Using this knowledge of how carefully Benjamin was protected, Joseph had a goblet secretly hidden in the youth's grainsack and accused him of stealing. When it was found, all the brothers returned to defend Benjamin. This concern for his own brother (Joseph was also Rachel's son) convinced him that at this late date they would no longer be jealous of him. (Gen. 35:16; 42–44)

Bethuel Be·thū'el

Bethuel was the son of Nahor, cousin of Abraham and father of Rebekah and Laban. He had probably died by the time of Rebekah's marriage to Isaac. (Gen. 22:22ff.)

Bildad Bil'dad

Bildad the Shuhite was one of Job's three friends who tried to comfort him in his troubles. (Job 2:11)

Bilhah Bil'hàh

Bilhah was a slave given to Rachel by her father at the time of her marriage to Jacob. In accordance with ancient custom, when Rachel found herself barren, she gave the slave to her husband as concubine. Bilhah bore Jacob two sons, Dan and Naphtali. (Gen. 29:29; 30:3, 5ff.)

Boaz Bō'az

Boaz was a wealthy landowner of Bethlehem and a relative of Naomi, mother-in-law of Ruth. At Naomi's suggestion, Ruth worked in his fields at harvest, gathering the grain left on the edges for the poor. Boaz noticed her, was reminded that he was a kinsman, and was happy to fulfill a kinsman's obligation toward a widowed relative by making her his wife.

Caesar Augustus Cae'sar Au·gus'tus *(see* **Augustus)**

Caiaphas Cā'ià·phàs

Caiaphas was appointed high priest in Jerusalem by Valarius Gratus in A.D. 18. He was deposed in A.D. 36. He suggested that Jesus might have to be killed in order to prevent trouble. Plans for the arrest were made in his house and the Sanhedrin held its hearing there. Caiaphas asked the key question about the messianic claims of Jesus, thereby encouraging the answer which led to the charge of blasphemy. Caiaphas appears later among the priests present at the trial of Peter and John in the early days of the church. His father-in-law, Annas, however, seems to have been the powerful figure behind whatever member of the family happened to be high priest at a particular time. (Matt. 26:3, 57; Luke 3:2; John 11:49–50; Acts 4:6)

Cain   Cāin

Cain was the first child of Adam and Eve and is identified with the farmer or peasant. When his grain offering to God was rejected in favor of the animal sacrifice of his brother, the shepherd Abel, he murdered Abel in envious rage. For this he was condemned to be a wanderer, and a special mark on his forehead protected him from danger as a fugitive. Cain built the first city and named it after his son Enoch, which means "foundation." (Gen. 4:1–17)

Caleb   Cā′leb

Caleb at the age of forty was chosen to represent the tribe of Judah as one of the twelve spies sent by Moses to scout the land of Canaan when the Israelites neared its border. The spies returned, reporting it to be a prosperous land but filled with warlike people. Caleb alone disagreed, assuring Moses that they would be well able to occupy the land. This counsel was rejected and the people settled in the wilderness for a generation. God had said that only Caleb and Joshua, who had shown sufficient trust to be willing to go forward, would eventually enter the Promised Land. Caleb again represented his tribe when Moses drew up an apportionment of the land at the time they were ready to enter. Joshua, however, became the leader under whom the land was conquered. When Caleb stood before him to receive the inheritance, he reminded Joshua of that moment, forty-five years earlier, when they had made the report. He was granted Hebron as his portion. (Num. 13:6; 14:6, 30; 26:65; 34:19; Josh. 14:6)

Cephas   Cē'phàs

"Cephas"—"rock"—is the Greek equivalent for "Peter," the surname given by Jesus to the disciple Simon. (*see also* **Peter**)

Christ   Chrīst

"Christ" is the Greek form for the title "Messiah," meaning "the anointed one." In the Scriptures, kings and priests were anointed to their office, signifying that they had been chosen by God. In later Scripture, "Messiah" also came to mean the promised one, the hoped-for deliverer whom God would send to save his people. When Christians called Jesus by the title "Christ," they were saying that he was the promised one called by God to save. (*see also* **Jesus**)

Cleopas   Clē′ȯ·pȧs

Cleopas was one of the two disciples who met the risen Lord on the resurrection day as they walked from Jerusalem to their home at Bethany. They talked with the stranger whom they met on the road, invited him to stay with them, and recognized him as he blessed bread and gave it to them. (Luke 24:18)

Crispus   Cris′pŭs

Crispus was a president of the synagogue in Corinth when Paul was living in the city and preaching there weekly. He and his family became Christians and when the believers were put out of the synagogue he followed with Paul to the home of Titius Justus. The Corinthian church grew in size, but Crispus was one of the few whom Paul himself baptized. (Acts 18:8; I Cor. 1:14)

Cyrus   Cy′rŭs

Cyrus II, called Cyrus the Great, was the founder of the Persian empire. Babylonia surrendered to him in 539 B.C. He was killed in battle in 529 B.C. In the Old Testament he is described as the one whom God has chosen to restore Israel, and this hope is fulfilled when he permits the Jews exiled in Babylon to return to Jerusalem to begin reconstruction of the temple. Whereas the Babylonians had deliberately deported conquered people, hoping thereby to destroy their identity, it was his policy to permit them to return to their own lands and to worship in their own way. Hence he sent back the sacred vessels to the temple. (Isa. 45:1; II Chron. 36:22ff.; Ezra 1; 6:16)

Dan Dăn

Dan was a son of Jacob and Bilhah, the slave of his wife Rachel. The name means "judgment" or "he who judges." One of the twelve tribes of Israel was named for Dan. (Gen. 30:6)

Daniel Dăn'iel

Daniel was a young man from among the nobility taken from Jerusalem after the siege of the city in 597 B.C. and carried captive to Babylon. King Nebuchadnezzar selected a group of these young men to be specially educated in Babylonian learning so that they would be competent to serve in his household. They were to eat the same food as royalty and were to continue their training for three years. Among this group were Daniel (given the Babylonian name of Belteshazzar) and three friends. They requested their trainer to permit them to eat simple food rather than the rich diet ordered by the king. They wished to keep the dietary rules of the Jewish Law but did not say so. The request was granted, although with concern that this might affect their health adversely. On the contrary, after three years on a diet of water and vegetables they made a better appearance than did those who had lived more indulgently. Moreover, their wisdom was greater than that of the king's magicians. This was indicated by Daniel's ability to interpret the king's dream, and to explain the mysterious handwriting of doom revealed on the wall during a feast.

The king had made a golden image of himself for worship to which Daniel and his friends refused to bow, and all were thrown into a furnace from which, to the king's relief, they emerged unscathed.

When Darius the Persian became king he divided his lands into satrapies, or provinces, and Daniel was chosen to become one of three presidents over the satraps. In this role he became so distinguished as to arouse the jealousy of others. They plotted his destruction by persuading the king to order that no one except himself should be worshiped. Daniel was seen, according to his custom, praying three times a day. For punishment he was thrown into a den of lions, from which he emerged unharmed. The king thereupon decreed the worship of Daniel's God. Thus Daniel was highly esteemed during the reign of two kings. (Daniel)

Darius Dà·rī′ús

Darius I was king of Persia 521–485 B.C. For many years he was at war with the Greek cities. Although he won a victory of Thermopylae, his army was defeated by the Athenians in the battle of Marathon, 490 B.C. Darius

I was the king under whom the rebuilding of the temple at Jerusalem was completed. His edict, sent with returning refugees, put an end to the local opposition which had kept the work incomplete. Darius' contribution to government was to divide his kingdom into satrapies, or provinces. The book of Daniel tells how Daniel was appointed one of three presidents over the satraps and how the king, incited by the jealousy of the others, was induced to declare himself as the only being worthy of worship. Daniel continued to worship God, was thrown to the lions, and remained unharmed, to the great relief of the king, who continued to honor him. (Ezra 4:24–6:22; Dan. 6)

Dathan Dā′thản *(see* **Moses***)*

David Dā′vid

David was the youngest of the eight sons of Jesse of Bethlehem. While still a youth herding his father's sheep, he was anointed by Samuel the prophet to become king of Israel. David first entered the service of King Saul when, bringing food to his soldier brothers, he took up the challenge of the Philistine Goliath and slew him with a slingshot. David immediately became popular, thereby arousing the jealousy of the king. He became a musician to the king, soothing with the sound of the lyre the disturbed moods which came upon Saul. He married the king's daughter, Michal, and became a close friend of the king's son Jonathan. Twice he had to flee the king's attempts to murder him, warned once by Michal, and once by Jonathan. First he fled to Ahimelech, priest of the sanctuary at Nod, who gave him the only food available, holy bread, and the sword of Goliath. He gathered about him a company of discontented men while hiding at the cave of Adullam. Saul sent an expedition to capture him, slaying the priests of Nod on the way because they had helped David, but David and his men hid in the wilderness of Judea. Twice David was close enough to the king to slay him but refused to do so. Then, fearing that Saul would finally capture him, he entered the service of the king of Gath for more than a year. However, at the insistence of the Philistine commanders, who did not trust him, David and his men remained away during the battle with Israel in which King Saul and his sons were killed.

David became king of Judah, reigning from Hebron, but remained at war with the house of Saul. Seven years later, after the murder of Saul's reigning son, David was offered the kingship by all the tribes of Israel. He captured the Jebusite city of Jerusalem and made it his capital, a strategic choice, since it had belonged neither to Israel nor to Judah. He brought the ark of the Lord into the city and gathered materials for the building of a temple, but this was not accomplished until after his death. According to the custom of his time, David had a large harem, but he incurred rebuke from the prophet Nathan when he took the wife of one of his army officers and had her husband killed in battle in order to conceal adultery.

The tragic domestic crisis of David's life was the revolt of his son Absalom. So successful was the young prince in gathering dissidents against the king, that David was forced to flee from Jerusalem. The revolt was eventually quelled and Absalom was killed. David mourned his son with such grief that his advisers had to warn him of his responsibilities toward those who had loyally fought in his behalf. This incident and that of a revolt in the tribe of Benjamin suggest that there was some dissatisfaction with his reign. A census which he made for purposes of taxation and conscription was deeply resented, and was affirmed by the prophet Dan to have brought about epidemic, famine, and revolt as a judgment of God. David firmly established the geographical boundaries of his kingdom, so successfully repelling some of the border nations that the Philistines, at least, were never again a military threat to Israel. When he died, he left the kingdom to Solomon, his second-oldest living son, child of Bathsheba. He lived at approximately 1000 B.C. and scholars believe that the material in II Sam. 9–20 was written by a contemporary. (I Sam. 16–31; II Sam.; I Kings 1–2:10; I Chron. 11–29)

Deborah   Deb'ŏ·ràh

Deborah, a prophetess, was a judge in Israel during the time of the settlement of the land. The people brought their quarrels to her and asked her to determine justice. When Jebin, king of Canaan, attacked her people with an army led by his commander, Sisera, Deborah summoned Barak to lead the men of Israel. The invading army was crushed; the leader and later the king were killed. The battle is remembered in the triumphant Song of Deborah in Judg. 5. (Judg. 4–5)

Delilah Dē·lī′lȧh

Delilah was loved by Samson, strong man and judge in Israel. Although probably an Israelite, she agreed to betray him to his enemies, the Philistines. She sought to know from him the secret of his strength. He evaded her three times with misleading answers, but finally disclosed that his secret was his uncut hair. She called men to cut off his hair while he slept, then woke him to deliver him into their hands. (Judg. 16:4–21)

Demas Dē′mȧs

Demas is mentioned by Paul in a letter written from prison in Rome to the church at Colossae and in a letter written during this same period to Philemon, who also lived at Colossae. This suggests that Demas was a worker in the church there. Demas may have visited Paul at Rome, but subsequently left, for Paul wrote to Timothy that Demas had deserted him and gone to Thessalonica, being in love with the world. (Col. 4:14; Philem. 24; II Tim. 4:10)

Dinah Dī′nȧh

Dinah was the only daughter of Jacob and Leah. When the tribe was settling in Canaan, she visited among the Canaanite women. She was seen by a tribal prince, Shechem, who raped her, fell in love, and asked for her as his wife. Her brothers, angered by this treatment of Dinah, plotted destruction. Naming circumcision as the price to be met for intermarriage, they carried off Dinah, killed the Canaanite men, and plundered the city. Jacob, fearing for his family's lives, left the area. (Gen. 30:21; 34)

Dorcas   Dôr′càs

Dorcas (or Tabitha in Hebrew) was a Christian disciple living at Joppa. She was renowned for her works of kindness, including the sewing of clothes for the needy. When she became sick and died, her friends, hearing that Peter was in a nearby town, sent for him. Peter ordered everyone to leave the room, prayed, and said to her, "Tabitha, rise." Tabitha's return to life caused rejoicing among the Christians and many people in Joppa became believers. (Acts 9:36–42)

Drusilla   Drü·sil′là *(see* **Felix***)*

Elah   Ē′làh *(see* **Omri***)*

Elhanan   El·hā′nàn *(see* **Goliath***)*

Eli   Ē′lī

Eli was priest in the sanctuary at Shiloh. The boy Samuel was entrusted to his care when his mother brought him, in fulfillment of her vow, to live in the service of the Lord. Eli's sons, who also served in the sanctuary, were notoriously high-handed in demanding more than their share from the sacrifices brought by the people, and this was considered to be blasphemy. The word of the Lord, coming to the boy Samuel, warned Eli of the judgment due his sons, and their descendants, for this sin. In a battle against the Philistines, the ark of the covenant was captured and Eli's sons, who had accompanied it, were killed. When Eli, old and blind, heard that the ark had been taken, he fell over and died. (I Sam. 1:1–4:18)

Elijah E·lī′jàh

Elijah is the prophet known initially for his constant opposition to the cult of Baal, which King Ahab had permitted his Phoenician wife Jezebel to introduce into Israel. He suddenly appeared before Ahab and predicted a three-year drought, then retired to a brook east of Jordan, beyond Ahab's domain. Later he withdrew to Zarephath in Sidon where he was housed and fed by a widow whose larder was continually refilled. When her son became ill and died, Elijah restored him. Finally Elijah returned to King Ahab and challenged the priests of Baal to end the drought. In a contest on Mount Carmel, the sacrifice to Baal never caught fire, while Elijah's sacrifice to the Lord was consumed. This indicated the superiority of Israel's God, for rain followed immediately upon the contest. Fleeing from Jezebel's wrath, Elijah hid in a cave on Mount Horeb, the sacred mountain, and there it was revealed to him that the word of God would not be made known in earthquake or fire but in a still voice. He was sent to anoint Hazael as the future king of Syria, Jehu as the future king of Israel, and Elisha as his successor as prophet. These three would work quietly for the destruction of Ahab's family. When Ahab confiscated Naboth's vinyard, Elijah reappeared at court to condemn this act against a fellow Israelite. Ahab repented.

Elijah reappears during the reign of the succeeding king, Ahaziah, condemning the ruler for seeking help of Baal-zebub, god of Ekron, instead of the Lord, when Ahaziah hoped for healing after a fall. At the end of his life he was accompanied by Elisha and a group known as "sons of the prophets" as he went from Gilgal across the Jordan River. When they had crossed, Elisha watched as his master was separated from him and went up in a whirlwind into heaven, leaving to his successor his mantle, his symbol of office. (I Kings 17–19; 21; II Kings 1:1–2:18)

Elimelech   E·lim'ė·lech *(see* **Ruth***)*

Elisha   E·lī'shå

Elisha was plowing his father's field when the prophet Elijah cast his mantle over the young man, signifying Elisha as his successor. Elisha accompanied Elijah on his final trip beyond the Jordan River and received from him promise of a double share of his spirit. After witnessing the translation of Elijah, he rejoined the company of prophets and was accepted by them as Elijah's successor. A series of wonder stories is recounted of him. Pouring salt into a spring, he so purified the water that the land became fertile. Pouring meal into a pot of poisonous stew, he purified the food. His curse destroyed some small boys who jeered at him. Answering the appeal of a widow in economic straits, he caused a jar of oil to multiply sufficiently so that her debts could be paid from the surplus. In a series of stories parallel to those told of Elijah, Elisha stayed in the guest room of a Shunammite couple, rewarded them with the promise of a son, and many years later, when the boy died, restored him to life. When Naaman, commander of the king of Syria's army, was sent to be healed of leprosy, Elisha bade the man bathe in the Jordan River and he was cured. Elisha refused reward, considering this his service to the Lord, and Naaman vowed to worship the God of Elisha.

King Jehoshaphat of Judah, concerned about the outcome of a war against Moab, sought the advice of Elisha and was assured of victory. At another time, Elisha warned the king of Israel to avoid a place to which the Syrian king was sending an army. The latter, wondering how the prophet found out such information, sent men to capture him. The raiding party were smitten with blindness, were led to the king of Israel, and, at Elisha's word, were released and returned to Syria. Once when the city of Samaria was gripped by famine during a siege by Syria, Elisha assured the king that the invading army would flee, and before morning this had happened. The Syrians, thinking they had heard the sounds of an attacking army, had decamped. One time when Elisha was at Damascus, the king of Syria, who was ill, sent a servant, Hazael, to inquire from the prophet about his recovery. Elisha told Hazael that he would become king of Syria and conquer Israel. Hazael returned to Damascus, smothered the king, and usurped the throne. Thus Elisha fomented revolt in Syria.

Several years later, Elisha called one of the prophet's group and sent him secretly to anoint Jehu as king of Israel and say that he was to destroy the family of Ahab. Jehu promptly informed his followers, who rallied around him to form a revolt. He slew King Jehoram of Israel and King Ahaziah of Judah, slew Jezebel at Jezreel (fulfilling the promise of Elijah), and ordered the death of all Ahab's sons. When Elisha lay dying, King Joash of Israel visited him and was promised three victories over Syria. So Elisha died and was buried by the prophets' group. He is remembered for his political activities and for stories of wonder-workings. (I Kings 19:19–21; II Kings 2:1–8:15; 9:1–3; 13:14–21)

Elizabeth   Ē·liz′à·bèth

Elizabeth was the wife of the priest Zechariah and bore him a child in her old age. The child, named John, became known later for his preaching and baptizing as a sign of repentance. She was a relative of Mary, who came to visit her when both women were pregnant. (Luke 1)

Elymas   El′y·màs *(see Sergius Paulus)*

Enoch   Ē′nòch

Enoch was the son of Cain for whom his father named a city. Another list names him as the son of Jared. It is said of him that he "walked with God" and that he did not die, but God took him. He may have been popular in tradition for he is mentioned in the apocryphal book of Ecclesiasticus among the famous men, in the genealogy of Jesus, and in the book of Hebrews among the men of faith. (Gen. 4:17ff.; 5:18; Ecclus. 44:16; Luke 3:37; Heb. 11:5)

Ephraim   Ē'phrà·im

Ephraim, the younger son of Joseph, was given the blessing of the elder son by his grandfather Jacob. In the distribution of land among the tribes in Israel, Joseph is represented by the two tribes of Ephraim and Manasseh, the former being larger. The name "Ephraim" is sometimes used by the prophets as a reference to the land of Israel. (Gen. 41:52; 46:20; 48:8–22)

Esau   Ē'sau

Esau, son of Isaac and Rebekah, was Jacob's twin. In the struggle of birth, Esau emerged first and thus became the elder son. A rough man and a huntsman, he so little prized his birthright that, returning hungry from a day's work, he sold it to his brother for a dish of stew. At the age of forty, Esau married two Hittite women instead of choosing a wife from among his own people, thus arousing bitterness with his parents. Nevertheless, Esau was the favorite son and Jacob enjoyed the meat provided from his hunting. When Jacob became old, he called Esau to bring him a favorite food and receive the blessing of the firstborn. But Jacob and Rebekah cunningly contrived to make Jacob the herdsman seem like his brother, and he received the blessing intended for Esau. This so angered Esau that Jacob was forced to flee. Esau, to please his father, then married one of the daughters of his uncle, Ishmael. Many years later, when Jacob and his family returned to Canaan, Esau, now a wealthy man, approached him with a company of four hundred men. Placated by gifts, however, Esau met his brother in a friendly way and invited him to live among his people in the land of Seir, an invitation prudently refused in the realization that the land could not adequately support both large families. The brothers met again at the funeral of their father, Isaac. In later literature, Esau is frequently identified with the land of Edom (Seir) to explain how the older nation could be subject to the younger nation, Israel. (Gen. 25:22–34; 26:34; 27; 35:29; 39:6–9)

Esther Ės'thėr

Esther's name is given to a book which recounts a deliverance of the Jewish people. When King Ahasuerus of Persia divorced his queen for refusing to appear at a banquet, he chose as her successor a young Jewish girl, Esther, whose Hebrew name was Hadassah. Her uncle and adoptive parent, Mordecai, discovered a plot of the grand vizier, Haman, to destroy their people, and persuaded Esther to risk her life by going unbidden into the king's presence to plead their cause. She first requested him and Haman to attend a banquet in her apartments. The king was gracious to her, visited, learned of the plot, and gave the Jews the right of self-defense against their enemies. So

Esther became an instrument for the providence of God. This story is the basis for the annual Jewish festival of Purim. (Esther)

Eunice Eu'nice

Eunice was a Jewish woman and Christian believer married to a Greek. She was the mother of Timothy, one of the friends of the apostle Paul. (Acts 16:1; II Tim. 1:5)

Eve Ēve

Eve is the name, explained as meaning the mother of all living, given to the first woman. Like man, she was created in the image of God and, coming from the rib of man, she was made of his flesh and able to be his partner. Eve was deceived by the serpent into eating fruit from the forbidden tree and she persuaded Adam, her husband, to do likewise. Together they shared the judgment of God that they would be banished from the garden. Her particular punishment was to have pain in childbirth and to become dominated by her husband. Eve was the mother of Cain and Abel. After the murder of Abel and Cain's banishment, she bore a third son, Seth. (Gen. 1:27; 2:18ff.; 3; 4:1, 25)

Ezekiel E·zēk'i·ėl

Ezekiel has given his name to a book in which his words to his people are written. He was a priest whose ministry was to the Jewish exiles in Babylon for about thirty years, from 593 to 563 B.C. His work was shaped by the fall of Jerusalem, forewarned in chapters 1 through 24. He had been deported with others to Babylon. While in exile, he warned of the judgment of God on other nations. The final chapters of the book bring hope and promise for the restoration of Israel, Jerusalem, and the temple.

Ezekiel discoursed in vivid symbols and taught through dramatic actions. There were times when he did not speak at all, letting his actions convey their own meaning. There were times when he went into ecstasies. More than other prophets, he insisted on the vision of the utter holiness of God, who would bring the nations to judgment. He also assured his people that God dwelt among them and ordered the events of their history. Brought up in a religion centered in the temple worship, his own responsibility was to assure his people that God also dwelt with them in Babylon. His words of promise helped to shape the form which Judaism would take after the restoration. He was concerned about the temple and the forms of worship there. Thus he prepared for the fulfillment of Nehemiah's work in the return to Jerusalem. (Ezekiel)

Ezra   Ėz′rà

Ezra was a priest during the Babylonian exile, well versed in the Law of Israel. King Artaxerxes of Persia, whose policy it was to allow subject peoples to preserve their own religion and customs, authorized him to return to Jerusalem with a group to restore the observance of their own Law. Some people had already returned, the temple had been rebuilt, and the walls reconstructed. The king sent with Ezra a gift of treasure, along with offerings from the Jewish people. This was in order that sacrifices could be offered and vessels made for temple ceremonies. After his arrival in Jerusalem, Ezra gathered the people together and read from a book the code of the Law, which was then explained by the Levites. There followed a celebration of the festival of Tabernacles, then a fast with confession of sins. Ezra was distressed to learn that Jews who had remained in their own land had intermarried with foreign women. They yielded to his plea to divorce those wives and give up the children of such marriages. Thus Ezra's work was to enforce a strict interpretation of the Law upon the people when they were beginning again their life in Jerusalem. (Ezra 7–10; Neh. 8–9)

Felix   Fē'lix

Marcus Antonius Felix, a freedman, was procurator of Judea, A.D. 52–59. He was in residence at Caesarea when the apostle Paul, after his arrest in Jerusalem, was brought there for safe-keeping. Felix and Drusilla (his second wife, who was Jewish) heard the case but had Paul returned to prison. Felix had hoped for a bribe but he also wanted to build favor with Jewish leaders by not closing the case. Felix was replaced in office and Paul remained in prison. His harsh rule caused insurrections among the Jews and was in large part responsible for the uprisings in 66–70 which finally led to the destruction of Jerusalem. (Acts 24)

Festus Fes'tŭs

Porcius Festus was appointed as successor to Felix as governor of Judea by the emperor Nero in A.D. 60. Paul, arrested in Jerusalem, was soon brought before him, and the apostle was offered a trial in Jerusalem. He refused and appealed to Caesar. Festus arranged a hearing for Paul before King Agrippa. Although the king would have acquitted him, the appeal to Caesar was overriding. Festus tried to pacify his resentful subjects but died in office after only two years. (Acts 24:27; 25; 26)

Gamaliel Gȧ'mā'li·ĕl

Gamaliel was a respected teacher of the Law in Jerusalem in New Testament times. The apostle Paul mentions that he was instructed by Gamaliel, which means that he received a formal education for several years in the content and interpretation of the Mosaic Law. Gamaliel was a member of the council when the apostles were brought there to answer for their preaching. The boldness of Peter aroused the anger of the council, members of which wanted to order their death. Gamaliel, in a closed session, cautioned reasonableness. He noted that other movements had arisen and died out and that the same might happen with the followers of Jesus. He warned that if their teaching did come from God, it would continue and the council might be opposing God. His advice was taken and the men were released. (Acts 22:3; 5:33–39)

Gedaliah   Ged·à·lī′àh

Gedaliah was appointed by King Nebuchadnezzar to be governor of Judea after the Babylonians had taken the city of Jerusalem and sent its wealthy people into exile. The people of the land remained and Gedaliah tried to reassure them, to bring orderly government, and to encourage them to return to their farms. The prophet Jeremiah was released from prison by the king's command and put into the safe-keeping of Gedaliah. He accepted the governor's offer to live near him. He had not been in office long before a member of the royal family with a small band of followers murdered Gedaliah. The rest of the community, fearful of reprisal, fled to Egypt. (II Kings 25:22–26; Jer. 39:11–14; 40:1–6)

Gideon   Gid′ē·òn

Gideon was one of the judges in Israel. At a time when the Israelite farmers were suffering from Midianite raids, Gideon, while working on his father's farm, heard the call of the Lord to end this oppression. Gideon protested his weakness and asked for a sign. This was given to him in the form of a sacrifice consumed by fire from the rock on

which it had been placed. Gideon's first act was to pull
down an altar to Baal on his father's land, and this aroused
the attention of his fellow townsmen. When the Midianites
next encamped in the Valley of Jezreel, Gideon called his
tribe to arms, but becoming fearful asked again for a sign
from God. This was given when dew appeared on a fleece
laid on dry ground, then as dew appearing on the ground
while the fleece remained dry. At God's command, Gideon
decreased his volunteers to a small disciplined army by
eliminating, first, all who were fearful, and then those who
indicated reluctance by kneeling to drink from a stream
instead of lapping up water as they ran. The hosts of
Midian were overcome by fear and confusion when Gideon
and his men surrounded their camp, blew trumpets,
smashed jars, and shouted their motto, "A sword for the
Lord and for Gideon." They pursued the Midianites, capturing other towns as they went. The Israelites invited
Gideon to be their ruler but he refused, saying that God
was their ruler. However, Gideon accepted gold from
among the spoils and made an ephod which he placed in
his city, Ophrah. (Judg. 6–9)

Goliath Gō·lī′áth

Goliath was a giant soldier of the Philistines, slain by
David in single combat. When the two armies were in their
camps, the challenge was sent out to settle the battle
through a contest between Goliath and anyone whom the
Israelites chose. The young David, armed only with a slingshot, accepted the challenge and slew the champion.

Another tradition names Elhanan of Bethlehem as Goliath's slayer, but the Chronicler says that he slew the brother of Goliath. (I Sam. 17; II Sam. 21:19; I Chron. 20:5)

Gomer   Gō′mér

Gomer was the wife of the prophet Hosea. As he describes their relationship, she had been a prostitute when he married her. She was the mother of three children, each named symbolically for the message the prophet had for Israel: a son, Jezreel; a daughter, Not Pitied; and a son, Not My People. Eventually Gomer left Hosea, but he bought her back publicly and ordered her to dwell in his house faithfully while he continued to be her husband. Thus Gomer symbolized the way in which Hosea saw Israel acting toward God. (Hos. 1:2ff.; 2:4ff.; 3:1–5)

Habakkuk   Hȧ·bak′kŭk

Habakkuk was a prophet who probably lived in the fifth century B.C. during the development of the Babylonian empire. Nothing is known of his life, but his thought is revealed in the brief book which bears his name. He addressed the problem of the justice of God, which seems to permit strong nations to conquer the weak. Habakkuk says with courage that each oppressive nation is eventually overcome by one stronger; that even under oppression the righteous person is vindicated by God; for God alone is the ultimate judge and ruler. (Habakkuk)

Hadasshah   Hà·dàs'sàh *(see* **Esther***)*

Hagar   Hā'gàr

Hagar was an Egyptian slave to Sarah, Abraham's wife. According to custom, Sarah, finding herself barren, gave Hagar to her husband as a concubine. Hagar conceived and immediately became contemptuous of her mistress. This angered Sarah, who so mistreated the slave that she fled. But the angel of the Lord met Hagar in her distress, told her to return, and promised fulfillment through her son. Hagar bore a son, Ishmael. Later, when Sarah's son was born, Sarah saw the two boys playing together and her jealousy was aroused. She asked and received reluctant permission from Abraham to banish both Hagar and Ishmael into the wilderness. There, when Hagar thought he would die of thirst, the angel again called to her in reassurance, and showed her a spring of water. So she brought up the boy in the wilderness of Paran. (Gen. 16:1–14; 21:9–21)

Haggai   Hag'gäi

Haggai was a prophet during the exile, of whom nothing is known except the writing in the book which bears his name, although he is mentioned in the book of Ezra. Concerned that the rebuilding of the temple lagged, Haggai urged Zerubbabel, governor of Judah, to hasten the completion of the work. Although it would not be as impressive as Solomon's temple, he wrote, it too would be filled with the glory of the Lord. Blessing would follow, both to the people of the land and to the family of Zerubbabel. The work is dated from August to December in the year 520 B.C. (Ezra 5:1; 6:14; Haggai)

Ham Hăm

Ham was the youngest of the three sons of Noah. After the flood, when Noah, a successful farmer, had drunk too much of his own wine, Ham discovered his father lying naked and told his brothers, who covered him. Upon awaking, Noah cursed Canaan through Ham their father. This seems to symbolize both the licentiousness of the land of Canaan and its eventual subjugation to Israel. (Gen. 5:32; 6:10; 7:13; 9:22–27)

Haman Hā'măn

Haman was promoted by King Ahasuerus of Persia to be grand vizier. All lower officials bowed down to him except Mordecai, a Jew, whose religion prohibited such reverence. This angered Haman, who persuaded the king to permit him to destroy all the Jews. The plot was brought to the attention of Queen Esther, who was Jewish, by her uncle, Mordecai. Haman was delighted to be invited to a banquet by the queen—only to learn there that Mordecai was to receive honors for his loyalty to the king. At a second banquet, Esther disclosed to the king, in Haman's presence, the plot to destroy the Jews. When the king angrily left the room, Haman threw himself on Esther, pleading for his life. The gesture was misinterpreted by the king, who immediately ordered Haman hanged from the gallows he had erected for Mordecai. (Esther 3–7)

Hananiah Han·à·nī'àh

(1) Hananiah was a prophet who had a dispute with the prophet Jeremiah over whether the alliance of King Zedekiah and others against Nebuchadnezzar would succeed. Jeremiah said it would not; Hananiah said it would. To prove his point, Jeremiah had put a yoke around his neck. Hananiah broke the yoke in their confrontation. Later Jeremiah predicted that Hananiah, a false prophet, would himself die shortly. That happened within the year. (Jer. 27–28)

(2) Hananiah was the Hebrew name of Shadrach. (*see also* **Shadrach**)

Hannah Hàn'nàh

Hannah was one of the two wives of Elkanah of Ephraim. She was the preferred wife, but she had no children. Each year, when the family went to sacrifice at the altar at Shiloh, she prayed in her distress. She vowed that if a son should be born to her, he would be dedicated to the Lord. Finally a son was born and while he was still small, she took him to Shiloh and gave him to the keeping of Eli, priest in charge of the ark and of the tabernacle there. Each year she visited him and brought him new clothes. Later she bore her husband three more sons and two daughters. (I Sam. 1; 2:1-21)

Hazael Haz′à·el *(see* **Elijah***)*

Herod Her′ŏd

(1) Herod, called the Great, was king of Judea, *c.* 37–34 B.C. Through his Idumean father, he was Jewish and this favored his rule iver the Jews. Early appointed procurator of Judea, his skillful diplomacy won the favor of successive Roman emperors despite the varying intrigues in Rome under Julius Caesar, Cassius, Mark Antony, and Augustus. Assisted by Roman legions, he won his kingdom from invading Parthians and across the years saw its boundaries increased through imperial favor to include Idumean Samaria, Galilee, Perea, and Bashan. A planner of cities, he rebuilt Caesarea, Jerusalem, and Jericho. He built fortified cities on the four sides of the Dead Sea. His family life was filled with intrigue and he had one wife, several sons, and other members of the family executed. While outwardly he observed the Jewish Law, he encouraged the spread of Roman culture. In spite of the prosperity he brought, his Jewish subjects hated him. It is consonant with his intense fear for his own life and power that he would have ordered the massacre of the infants of Bethlehem near the end of his own reign. (Matt. 2; Luke 1:5)

(2) Herod Antipas, son of Herod the Great by Malthace, ruled Galilee and Perea as tetrarch. When he divorced his

first wife to marry Herodias, he incurred not only scandal among the Jews but the anger of his former father-in-law, King Aretas of the Nabateans, who later declared war. When John the Baptist voiced condemnation, Herod imprisoned and executed him. Jesus indicated his scorn of the king once by defying a warning that Herod sought his death, and later by refusing to speak when, a prisoner, he was sent by Pilate to Herod as a courtesy to the ruler of Galilee. Herod was used as a spy by the emperor Tiberias, at whose death Herod went to Rome to seek honors from the new emperor, Caligula. But King Agrippa sent charges against him and Herod was banished to Lyons (A.D. 40), where he was accompanied by his wife Herodias. (Matt. 14:3–12; Mark 6:14–29; Luke 13:31–32; 23:6–12)
Pick up page 103

(3) Herod Agrippa was a grandson of Herod the Great and Mariamne and the son of Aristobulus. He became Herod Agrippa I. Born in Rome in 10 B.C., he became a friend of Caligula, who rewarded him with the territories of Galilee, Judea, and Samaria. Although thoroughly a part of Hellenic culture, he zealously observed the Jewish Law, thus becoming popular with the Pharisees. He persecuted the Christian community in Jerusalem, authorizing the death of James and imprisoning Peter and other apostles. After a brief reign, A.D. 41–44, he died suddenly in the midst of a public ceremony. (Acts 12:1–20)

Hezekiah Hez·é·kī′áh

Hezekiah was twenty-five years old when he became king of Judah and reigned for twenty-nine years (716–

687 B.C.). He is remembered as a king who removed idols and tried to keep the commandments of God. He revived the temple sacrifices and tried to make Jerusalem the center for worship. Always troubled by the threat of invasion, he sought advice from the prophet Isaiah, but the two disagreed on how much trust one could place on kingly alliances, for Hezekiah turned first to Egypt, then to Babylon for help against Assyria. Early in his reign, Samaria, capital of Israel, was conquered by the king of Assyria and the people were sent into exile. Hezekiah tried to buy off Sennacherib by paying tribute, even stripping the temple of its gold and silver. In spite of this, the emissaries of Assyria taunted Hezekiah for his alliance with the king of Egypt, and eventually an army was drawn up before the gates of Jerusalem. Then, suddenly, hundreds among the troops died, probably of pestilence, and the army withdrew. At another time, envoys from Babylon came to Hezekiah seeking mutual alliance against the Assyrians. Hezekiah entertained them, even to displaying the extent of his treasure, which brought rebuke from Isaiah, who told him that this would only arouse the envy of the visitors. In order to protect his city against attack, he strengthened its walls and towers, and collected water from springs outside the city into an aqueduct which brought water inside the walls, where it would be more available in case of siege. At one time Hezekiah became ill and thought he was near death. He prayed for deliverance and Isaiah assured him that because of his righteousness, he

would be spared. He reigned fifteen years longer. (II Kings
18–20; II Chron. 29–32; Isa. 20; 36–39)

Hiram   Hī'ràm

Hiram, king of Tyre from 969 to 953 B.C., was friend
both to King David and to David's son Solomon. Hiram
provided the materials, principally timber, gold, and skil'ed
craftsmen, that enabled David to build himself a palace,
and Solomon to build the temple, as well as a larger palace
and other elaborate works in Jerusalem. This was paid for
at first in grain, wine, and oil, but Hiram did not find the
payment sufficient. Solomon then ceded twenty Galilean
cities and when the king still complained he added 120
gold talents. Hiram and Solomon conducted joint trade
ventures with Orphir in Arabia and on the Red Sea, the
ships and sailors being supplied by the king of Tyre. He
began the outreach into other Mediterranean areas leading
to more trade and colonization. (II Sam. 5:11; I Kings 5;
9:10–14; 10:11–13; I Chron. 14:1ff.; II Chron. 2:1–16;
8:2)

Hosea   Hō·śē'à

Hosea was the prophet native to Israel who spoke to his
own people in the time of deep distress immediately fol-
lowing the prosperity which Amos had rebuked. The
Assyrians had conquered nearby areas and threatened
Israel's capital, Samaria, which they finally captured in 721
B.C. Four kings were assassinated in quick succession.
Hosea's book describes the sufferings of Israel as caused by

faithlessness to her covenant with Yahweh. This is dramatized by parallel references to Hosea's own marriage. Instructed by the Lord, he had married a prostitute, Gomer, and it was not certain that the three children whom she bore were his. He named them Jezreel (for blood shed there by Jehu, Israel would be punished), Not Pitied, and Not My People. Gomer left him, but, still instructed by God, he openly bought her back. So Hosea, through the constant pain of a faithless marriage, himself felt and proclaimed the pain and anger of God whose people had turned away from him but who still hoped to redeem and restore Israel. (Hosea)

Hoshea Hō·shē′ȧ

Hoshea became the last king of Israel by assassinating his predecessor, Pekah, and being installed as a puppet ruler by Tiglath-pileser of Assyria, who had conquered the area. He continued this role for about eight years but then refused to pay tribute and turned to the Egyptians for an alliance. Shalmaneser promptly imprisoned Hoshea and laid siege to the city of Samaria. After three years it was captured and the people of Israel were scattered forever. (II Kings 15:30; 17:1–6)

Hushai Hū′shäi *(see* **Absalom***)*

Isaac   Ī'saac

Isaac's name means "he who laughs" and this may refer either to his mother's unbelieving laughter when told that she would bear a son in her old age, or to the joy of Abraham and Sarah when the son was born who was to inherit the promise. On the day of his weaning, Abraham gave a feast in celebration. As a young boy, Isaac accompanied his father on a three-day journey to Mount Moriah for sacrifice. Arriving there, Isaac learned that he was to be the sacrifice. Assured that God would provide the sacrifice, he was bound and laid upon the wood of the altar. But just before he was to be slain, the angel of the Lord called to Abraham, staying his hand, and indicating a ram caught in a nearby thicket. Abraham had demonstrated obedience, Isaac had submitted, and God, accepting this token of faithfulness, reiterated the promise of blessing through the son.

When Isaac was grown, and shortly after the death of Sarah, Abraham sent a trusted servant to Mesopotamia to the house of his brother Nahor, where he won the consent of the daughter, Rebekah, to return to be Isaac's bride. It was a number of years, however, before she bore twin sons, Jacob and Esau. Rivalry between the sons reached a climax when Jacob, aided by Rebekah to simulate the appearance of Esau, deceived his father into giving him the blessing of the firstborn which Isaac had intended for Esau. Isaac had been unhappy when Esau had married Hittite wives, so now he and Rebekah sent Jacob to her father's family to find a wife, as well as to escape Esau's anger.

In a time of famine, Isaac had settled in the land of the Philistines, but his growing prosperity there aroused envy. When he moved into another area, there were quarrels over wells dug in his father's time to which he now tried to return. Finally the offer of a treaty of friendship with Abimelech, king of the Philistines, assured him peace. When Isaac died at an advanced age, both his sons had become reconciled and he was buried in the family tomb at Hebron. (Gen. 18:1-17; 21:1-8; 22:1-14; 24; 25:19-26; 26-27; 28:1-5; 35:27-29)

Isaiah　Ī·sāi′ăh

Isaiah lived in Jerusalem during the reign of King Hezekiah, probably speaking the words written in his book between 742–687 B.C. This makes him a contemporary of Amos, Hosea, and Micah, all of whom were warning their people in a troubled time. Isaiah was married and had two sons. Because of his closeness to the court, and his familiarity with the king, it is thought that he belonged to the nobility. His presence in the temple suggests also that he was a priest. Isaiah lived during the time of the Assyrian conquest of the sister nation, Israel, and saw his own land constantly invaded.

Isaiah received his call to be a prophet in a vision of the glory of the Lord while in the temple. Protesting his inadequacy, he received the assurance of the forgiveness of sin and accepted the commission. Isaiah's words affirmed the utter holiness of God, whose purposes transcended the plans of nations. Remembering that Judah was bound to God in an everlasting covenant, he tried to persuade the king not to trust in political alliances with neighboring Egypt and Babylon. He tried to prevent revolt against Sennacherib and could only watch as fortified cities were taken and heavy tribute was exacted. To Isaiah, these humiliations were the judgment of God on his people for their lack of trust. He was able to assure them that the city of Jerusalem itself would be spared, and he saw a time when the Assyrian armies decamped from its gates. King Hezekiah was rebuked another time by Isaiah when a generous impulse led him to reveal his treasures to visiting emissaries from Babylon. He reassured the king of restored health at a time of serious illness.

Isaiah's efforts to persuade the king of Judah to live only by trusting in the covenant with God never received much support. He lived at a time when the land was subject to a foreign power but he did not live to see the destruction of Jerusalem. His words have been a universal affirmation of the holiness and righteousness of God. While he warns of the destruction of nations because of their evil ways, he proclaims that the purposes of God will be fulfilled. The nations of earth will be judged and those who repent will be saved. God alone is to be trusted. (Isa. 1–39)

Iscariot *(see* **Judas Iscariot***)*

Ish-bosheth   Ish-bō′sheth

Ish-bosheth, son of Saul, was made king in his father's place by Abner, commander of the army. Ish-bosheth was forty years old and reigned for two years. David at that time ruled Judah from Hebron. There was constant war between the two armies, with David growing stronger and Ish-bosheth growing weaker. Matters reached a climax when the king rebuked his commander, Abner, for taking one of Saul's concubines, thereby violating royal prerogative. This so angered Abner that he asked King David to negotiate a surrender. An agreement was made. But Joab, David's commander, heard of it and, distrusting Abner, assassinated him. This news dismayed Ish-bosheth, who knew that no one could save his throne. One day while he was taking a noonday rest in his house, two bandit leaders from his own people crept in and killed him, taking his head to David in hope of reward. But David ordered their deaths and buried Ish-bosheth at Hebron. (II Sam. 2:8–4)

Ishmael   Ish′mà·el

Ishmael was the son of Abraham by his concubine Hagar, an Egyptian and slave of his wife, Sarah. Because he was the firstborn son, he aroused the jealousy of Sarah. When she saw him playing with her smaller son one day, she expelled both Hagar and Ishmael. They nearly died in the wilderness until a well was discovered. Ishmael grew up

in the wilderness of Paran and he became a skilled hunter.
He married a wife from Egypt. His sons formed nomadic
tribes living in areas bordering Israel. (Gen. 6:11–14;
17:15–18)

Israel   Is′ra·el *(see Jacob)*

Jabal   Jābål *(see Tubal-cain)*

Jacob   Jā′cob

Jacob was one of the twin sons of Isaac and Rebekah.
Although the second to be born, he managed to obtain
the right of succession to his father. When his huntsman
brother, Esau, came home hungry one day, Jacob gave him
a stew he was cooking in return for the promise of his
birthright. Since Jacob was the favorite of his mother, she
contrived to help him simulate the hairiness of Esau in
order to deceive the father and gain the firstborn's blessing
which had been intended for the elder. Now he was in
danger from his brother's anger, and his mother suggested
to Isaac that the young man visit her family to find a wife
among their kin. Lonely at the start of his exile, he dreamed
of a ladder reaching to heaven and the word of the Lord
reaffirmed the covenant made with Abraham, assuring him

of God's continuing presence. Jacob made an altar there and called it Bethel. He continued to Haran, where he agreed to serve his uncle, Laban, seven years in return for receiving his younger daughter, Rachel, for wife. However, Laban substituted the older daughter, Leah, and insisted that this was not deception but the local custom that the firstborn be the first married. So Jacob received two wives and worked fourteen years with Laban. Leah, the unwanted wife, bore Jacob four sons, to the envy of Rachel. Rachel gave Jacob her servant Bilhah as concubine, who bore two sons. Leah, not to be outdone, gave him her maid Zilpah, who also bore two sons. Leah again bore two sons and a daughter. Finally Rachel bore Joseph.

After twenty years in Haran, Jacob, who, partly by trickery, had accumulated wealth, departed without notice. Laban pursued him to ask why he had left in such haste. In the hill country of Gilead he caught up with Jacob, who insisted that he wanted to return to his own land. The two families made a covenant protecting the rights of Laban's daughters and each family went its own way. Jacob next turned to the problem of meeting Esau. He sent messengers ahead. They returned with the message that Esau was coming with four hundred men. Jacob sent ahead hundreds of animals as gifts, then sent his family. All night he wrestled with an angel, receiving finally the blessing of a new name, Israel (meaning "he who strives with God.") Esau received his brother generously and offered to share land with him, but Jacob thought it wiser to find a place for himself. He was still journeying when Rachel gave birth to her second son, Benjamin. Rachel did not survive the childbirth and was buried on the way to Ephroth. So Jacob had twelve sons and one daughter. He settled in the land of Canaan. Joseph was his favorite son. When the young boy was spirited away by jealous brothers and sold into slavery, Jacob mourned him, believing him to be dead. Years later, when the sons had sought food from Egypt in time of famine, he learned that Joseph was alive. Jacob spent his final years in Egypt, settling with his family in Goshen. He died there and was embalmed, and Joseph accompanied his body to the family burial place at Hebron. (Gen. 25:21–34; 27–37; 45:24–46:7; 47:27–50:15)

Jael Jā'ĕl

Jael was the wife of Heber the Kenite in the days when the tribes of Israel were being oppressed by the king of Canaan. When Sisera, commander of the Canaanite troops, retreated from the attack by Barak, the Israelite commander, he took refuge in the tent of Jael, who offered him hospitality. She fed him and he asked her to stand guard at the entrance to the tent while he slept. But instead, Jael, whose people were related to the Israelite tribes, drove a tent peg into his head with a hammer while he slept. When Barak appeared in pursuit, she went to meet him and led him to his dead enemy. (Judg. 4:17ff.; 5:6, 24ff.)

James Jāmes

(1) James, son of Zebedee and brother of John, was called from his fishing boat by Jesus to become one of the twelve disciples. The two brothers continued with Jesus to

Capernaum and were with him at Peter's house there. James belonged to an inner group of three (with Peter and John) who witnessed events to which the others were not invited: the raising of Jairus' daughter, the transfiguration, and the agony in Gethsemene. James and John (or their mother) once asked Jesus if they might have the seats of honor when he came into his kingdom and he, replying, asked if they could drink the cup he was ready to drink. They said that they could. The others were angry at this play for power. As they traveled toward Jerusalem, a Samaritan village refused entrance to the tired Jewish travelers, and James and John asked Jesus to call down lightning to strike them. This may be why Jesus named them "sons of thunder" (Boanerges). An active leader in the early church, James was killed in a persecution by King Herod Agrippa, A.D. 42. (Mark 1:19,29; 5:37; 9:2; 10:35ff.; 14:33; Luke 9:54; Acts 12:1–2)

(2) James, son of Alphaeus, is simply mentioned in lists of the disciples as one of the Twelve. (Mark 3:18)

(3) James "the brother of the Lord," was the brother of Joseph, Simon, and Judas of Nazareth. It is said that the brothers of Jesus opposed his ministry and at one time tried to stop him. Yet James appears in the book of Acts as head of the Christian community, and Paul notes that James was the only person he saw, in addition to Peter, the first time he went to Jerusalem as a believer. He says elsewhere that James was one of the persons who saw an appearance of the risen Lord. When the council at Jerusalem discussed the matter of how Gentiles were to be

received into the Christian community, James urged that they simply be enjoined to keep the basic elements of the Law regarding idolatry, unchastity, and certain food regulations. Paul later reported to James and the others on the success of his mission to the Gentiles. He is thought to have been martyred in an early persecution. (Matt. 13:55; Mark 6:3; Acts 12:17; 15:13–23; 21:18; Gal. 1:19; 2:9; I Cor. 15:7)

Japheth Jā′pheth

Japheth was the third son of Noah. He was in the ark, and he returned to settle the land. (Gen. 9:27)

Jared Jâr′ĕd *(see* **Enoch***)*

Jedidiah Jed·i·dī′ăh *(see* **Solomon***)*

Jehoahaz Jehō′à·haz

(1) Jehoahaz was the son of Jehu, the man who had usurped the throne of Israel from the family of King Ahab. As in his father's time, the land of Israel was constantly being invaded by the Syrians under Hazael and his son Benhadad. Finally deliverance and peace came. Jehoahaz permitted idolatry to continue as it had under previous kings. He reigned for seventeen years, 815–801 B.C. (II Kings 10:35; 13:1–9)

(2) Jehoahaz, son of Josiah, reigned as king of Judah for three months in 609 B.C. Josiah had been defeated and slain by Pharaoh Neco in the battle of Mediggo, and the people of Judah then made his son king. But Pharaoh Neco

captured him, deposed him, imprisoned him at Riblah, and finally sent him in chains to Egypt where he died. (II Kings 23:30–35)

Jehoash   Je·hō'ash

(1) Jehoash (also called Joash) was the only son of King Ahaziah of Judah who survived when the king's mother, Athaliah, destroyed the royal family. The child's aunt, Jehosheba, half-sister of Ahaziah and wife of the chief priest, Jehoiada, abducted him and hid him for six years in the temple. After that time, Jehoiada showed the boy to the palace guard and asked that they protect him. Thus surrounded, he was anointed king. The guards then turned on Athaliah and killed her. Jehoiada renewed the covenant between God and the king and the people. Idolatry was removed. The land was at peace. Jehoash ordered that offerings be used for repairs to the temple, but when no work was accomplished, a money chest was set up, the offerings were given to the workmen, and the work was finally accomplished. Judah was invaded by King Hazael of Syria, but before he reached the gates of Jerusalem, Jehoash bought him off by sending both the temple treasure and the palace treasure as tribute. The king had two wives and many children. He reigned nearly forty years (837–800 B.C.) and was assassinated in a conspiracy. (II Kings 11–12; II Chron. 22:10–24).

(2) Jehoash, son of Jehoahaz, was king of Israel, 801–786 B.C. Visiting the prophet Elisha at a time when the country was threatened by Syrian invasion, he was assured

of a triple victory. Three times during his reign, King Jehoash was able to recapture cities and defeat the kings of Syria. Challenged by King Amaziah of Judah, Jehoash captured the neighboring king, broke down the walls of Jerusalem, and took spoils from the temple and the palace. (II Kings 13:10–14:16)

Jehoiachin Je·hoi'å·chin

Jehoiachin was the son of Jehoaikim, king of Judah at the time of its capture by the Babylonians in 597 B.C. The father had revolted after three years of vassalage but died before King Nebuchadnezzar appeared. Jehoiachin, at the age of eighteen, was king of Judah for three months, but when the Babylonians laid siege to Jerusalem, the city immediately surrendered. He, with the rest of the royal family, was deported to Babylon, where he was permitted to live in some comfort. (II Kings 24:6–16; II Chron. 36:9ff.)

Jehoiada Je·hoi'å·då

Jehoiada was a priest in the temple of Jerusalem and husband of Jehosheba, a member of the royal family who saved the young prince Jehoash. Jehoiada hid him in the temple for six years, arranged for the temple guard to protect him while the priest anointed the boy king, and incited the murder of the usurping queen, Athaliah. He was regent and adviser to the young king during his minority. Jehoiada was responsible for the renewal of the covenant between God and the king and the people of Judah.

He was charged with repair of the temple, but there seems to have been some question about delays and misuse of money. The work was finally completed. (II Kings 11:1–20; 12:7ff.)

Jehoiakim Je·hoi′a·kim

Jehoiakim, son of King Josiah, became king of Judah after Pharaoh Neco of Egypt, who controlled Judah, deposed his brother Jehoahaz. Jehoiakim was twenty-five years old at the time of his accession and reigned 609–598 B.C. During this time, Egypt was conquered by the rising power of Babylon and her vassal states then came under the rule of King Nebuchadnezzar. After three years, Jehoiakim revolted, but died before the Babylonian army arrived.

Jehoiakim aroused the anger of the prophet Jeremiah, who accused him of oppression for personal gain. Early in the king's reign, Jeremiah had spoken in the temple court, warning of judgment, and was tried for treason but acquitted. Years later, when Jeremiah's woes against Jerusalem were read to the people by his secretary, Baruch, on a fast day proclaimed as the Babylonian army threatened, the princes asked to hear it read privately. They then cautioned Jeremiah and Baruch to hide while they had the scroll read to the king. The king burned the pages one by one, thus defying the warning of the Lord through the prophet. (II Kings 24:1–; II Chron. 36:5–8; Jer. 22:18ff.; 26:1–19; 36:1–27; 26:20–25)

Jehoram Je·hō′ràm

(1) Jehoram (also written Joram) was a son of Ahab and brother of Ahaziah, whom he succeeded as king of Israel. He reigned from 849 to 842 B.C. When the king of Moab, a vassal, revolted, refusing to send the annual tribute of sheep and wool, Jehoram called to his aid two other vassals, the kings of Judah and Edom. After a seven-day march, they could find no water, but upon inquiring of the prophet Elisha, were assured that they would be saved. Water was found in the mountains and the king of Edom conquered in battle. At another time, Jehoram made war against King Hazael of Syria and was wounded. He returned to Jezreel to convalesce. There word was given him that Jehu, incited by the prophet Elisha, was on his way to destroy the house of Ahab. Jehoram went out to meet the usurper, and was slain in Naboth's vineyard, fulfilling an oracle made when Ahab had confiscated the land. (II Kings 1:17; 3:1-3; 8:28-9:29; II Chron. 22:5-9)

(2) Jehoram was a king of Judah whose reign partially overlapped that of a king of Israel by the same name. Jehoram, who reigned 849-842 B.C., was the son of King Jehoshaphat and married to Athaliah, daughter of Ahab and Jezebel. He was thirty-two years old when he became king. It is said that he killed all his brothers and some of the other princes at the time of his accession. Edom, a vassal state, successfully revolted, as did Libnah. Both the Philistines and the Arabs invaded Jerusalem and carried away

not only his treasure but members of the royal household
He was so disliked that he was denied the funeral of kings
and although buried in Jerusalem was not laid in the tombs
of the kings. (I Kings 22:51; II Kings 8:16–24; II Chron.
21)

Jehoshaphat   Je·hosh′à·phat

Jehoshaphat was king of Judah from 873 to 849 B.C.
He was thirty-five years old at the beginning of his reign.
Jehoshaphat joined Ahab, the king of Israel, in war against
Syria, but first insisted that the prophets be consulted. Only
one, Micaiah, refused to promise victory, and Jehoshaphat
went with reservations. The king of Israel, although disguised, was killed, but Jehoshaphat was recognized and
spared. In the eighteenth year of his reign he again joined
Israel, under King Jehoram, in a more successful fight
against the king of Moab. Jehoshaphat tried to revive the
trade with Ophir for gold, which Solomon had earlier
established, but the first ships were wrecked. King Ahaziah
of Israel offered to join him in the venture, but Jehoshaphat preferred to give up the idea. He successfully fortified
cities in Judah, received tribute from the Philistines and the
Arabs, and lived in peace for many years. He restored the
worship of God, sent teachers among the people, and
appointed judges. He was regarded as a good king. (I Kings
15:24; 22; II Kings 3; II Chron. 17–20)

Jehosheba   Je·hosh′e·bà *(see* **Jehoiada***)*

Jehu Jē′hū

Jehu was designated by the prophet Elijah to destroy the house of Ahab. The commission was carried out by his successor, Elisha, who sent one of his prophet band to anoint Jehu, a commander of the army, as king of Israel. Jehu, called from his fellows for this symbolic act, returned to tell them of it carelessly. They, however, acknowledged the anointing and a conspiracy against King Jehoram began. Jehu rode furiously toward the king, who was at Jezreel recovering from battle wounds, and killed him in personal combat. The king of Judah, who had been an ally of Jehoram, was pursued and killed. Jehu returned to Jezreel and ordered Queen Jezebel thrown from a window. When the people of Samaria, capital of Israel, sued for peace, Jehu demanded the heads of the king's seventy sons. Jehu assembled the people of Samaria and craftily proclaimed a solemn assembly to Baal and attended the sacrifices himself; but he had previously arranged to have the temple surrounded by armed guards, who slew all the worshipers as they emerged. His was a bloody accession of power but the Chronicler commends him for destroying the cult of Baal and the impious house of Ahab. He reigned for twenty-eight years (842–815 B.C. and nothing is said of the rest of his rule. (I Kings 19:16ff.; II Kings 9:1–10:35)

Jephthah Jeph′thàh

Jephthah was one of the judges at the time the tribes of Israel were settling in Canaan. An illegitimate son, he was driven from his father's house by his stepbrothers to prevent his sharing the inheritance. He settled in the land of Tob and gathered around himself a robber band. When Gilead, his native land, was being oppressed by the Ammonites, the elders recalled Jephthah and asked him to lead in the struggle against the Ammonites. Scorning them at first because they had exiled him, he agreed to lead the battle, provided that upon a successful completion of the campaign he might become their ruler. The elders agreed. Jephthah sent his challenge to the king of Ammon and, as he went into battle, vowed to sacrifice to God whatever first met him on his return. His army subdued the Ammonites and he returned to Gilead victorious, to be greeted first by his only child, a daughter. Sorrowfully he told her of the vow and granted her two months to go into the wilderness with her companions to mourn her unmarried state. Human sacrifice was still accepted in Israel at that time. The Ephraimites complained that they had not been invited to join in the battle against Ammon, thus provoking a war in which they were badly defeated. Jephthah was a ruler in Israel for six years. (Judg. 10:5–11:11)

Jeremiah   Jer·e·mī′ah

Jeremiah the prophet was born into a priestly family at Anathoth near Jerusalem around 650 B.C. While he was still young he felt called to be the Lord's spokesman to Judah, and his vocation was carried on through the reigns of four kings. While Josiah was king, strong religious reforms were made, but he was killed in battle by Pharoah

Neco of Egypt, and his son Jehoahaz was deposed after three months in favor of a brother, Jehoiakim. At this time, Assyria had been overcome by Babylon, and the Egyptians decisively defeated. Jeremiah saw the eventual triumph of Babylon as master of the entire region and therefore the agent through whom the Lord would punish his people for their faithlessness. This branded him a Babylonian sympathizer and brought bitter hatred from the king. Jeremiah did not marry because he thought that children would not survive the judgment. Yet during the siege of Jerusalem he bought ancestral land in Anathoth as a symbol of restoration. There were conspiracies against his life, and he was confined to the stocks in the temple for a night because he warned of the destruction of the city. Early in Jehoiakim's reign, Jeremiah stood in the temple court exhorting the people to repentance and warning of their destruction. He was brought to trial for these words but released. One of his rebukes to the king for his personal injustices is found in Jer. 22:1–23.

In 605 Jeremiah dictated all he had spoken up to that time to his secretary, Baruch, who wrote his messages on a scroll. This was read to the people gathered in the temple court, then to the royal officers who had requested a private hearing. They sent Jeremiah and Baruch into hiding while they presented the scroll before King Jehoiakim. As the king listened to the warning that Babylon would conquer his kingdom, he cut up the scroll column by column and threw it on the fire. Jeremiah's response was to dictate a longer scroll.

During Zedekiah's three-year reign as a vassal of Babylon, the king consulted Jeremiah frequently but was influenced by his officers, who felt that Jeremiah's words broke down the morale of the people. Jerusalem was under siege, but when the Babylonian army had withdrawn at the approach of the Egyptians, Jeremiah left the city and was arrested on suspicion of desertion. The king saved him from death but kept him under house arrest. The Babylonians finally entered the city, carrying the king and nobility into exile. But at Ramah, Jeremiah's release was ordered, and he was given a choice of going to Babylon or of remaining in Judah. He chose the latter and was placed under the care of the governor, Gedaliah, at Mizpah. He urged his captive people to serve the king of Babylon. After the assassination of Gedaliah, the people, fearing reprisals from Babylon, asked Jeremiah if they should flee to Egypt. He warned against this, but they refused his word angrily, forcing him and Baruch to go with them. He warned that Egypt also would be conquered by Babylon, and he rebuked his people for idolatry in Egypt. It is supposed that he died there. (Autobiographical material in Jer. 1–22; biographical, 26–45)

Jeroboam Jer·ȯ·bō′ȧm

(1) Jeroboam I was noticed by King Solomon as an able young man and placed in charge of forced labor in one of the tribes, possibly Ephraim or Manasseh. One day as he was leaving Jerusalem, the prophet Ahijah met him, removed a new garment which he tore into twelve strips,

and invited Jeroboam to take ten as a symbol that he would rule over most of Solomon's kingdom. He was in exile in Egypt, perhaps because the king suspected him of fomenting revolt, at the time of Solomon's death when Rehoboam went to Shechem expecting to be made king. But Jeroboam, returning, became spokesman for the people in demanding that Rehoboam lighten the harsh yoke of taxation and forced labor that his father had imposed upon them. Rehoboam, consulting with his young nobles, replied that he would oppress them more than had his father. The representatives of Israel departed, but when Rehoboam began to fulfill his word, they revolted and made Jeroboam their king. From that time on, only Judah and Benjamin were ruled by the house of David. Jeroboam built his capital at Shechem. Fearful that his people might continue to look on Jerusalem as the center for worship, he made two golden calves which he set up, one in Bethel and one in Dan. Thus he encouraged idolatry. Once, when his son lay ill, he sent his wife to the prophet Ahijah, who announced that not only would the boy die, but that he would be the only son of the house of Jeroboam to die naturally. The house of Jeroboam was to be punished for idolatry. Jerobaom reigned from 922 to 901 B.C. (I Kings 11:26–14:20)

(2) Jeroboam II was king of Israel 786–746 B.C. During his long reign he restored the borders of Israel to their largest extent, from Hamath to the Arabian Sea, even capturing Damascus. He was a contemporary of Hosea and Amos. Amos, threatening the destruction of Jeroboam's family, was ejected from the shrine at Bethel by command

of the king. (II Kings 13:13; 14:23-29; Amos 7:9-11; Hosea 1:1)

Jesse Jes'se

Jesse lived in Bethlehem and kept flocks of sheep. He had seven sons, one of whom, David, was anointed by Samuel to become king of Israel. When David was an outlaw from King Saul, he took his parents to Moab for safety. (I Sam. 16:5ff.; 23:3ff.)

Jesus Jē'sùs

Jesus (Hebrew name: Joshua) was the son of Mary of Nazareth, married to a carpenter, Joseph. At this time, about 4 B.C., Caesar Augustus had ordered a census throughout the empire, and the couple had gone to Bethlehem, Joseph's ancestral home (he was of the Davidic family) to register. Soon after the child's birth, concerned by rumors that King Herod's fear of a supplanter would cause the massacre of infants in the area, they fled to Egypt and eventually returned to Nazareth where Jesus grew up, and came to be known as the carpenter. When he was about twelve years old, following custom, he accompanied Mary and Joseph to Jerusalem for Passover and probably his own bar mitzvah, since the account tells of his hearing and asking questions of the rabbis.

Jesus next appears at about the age of thirty when he joined the crowds in southern Judea listening to his cousin John preaching repentance and was baptized by John in the Jordan River. He went into the wilderness nearby for a period of inner struggle, evidently connected with the form of his calling, which seemed to him a temptation. When he emerged, he returned to Galilee where he called twelve men to accompany him as he went among the villages announcing his message of the kingdom of God. He affirmed that he was sent by God and indicated this by the power of God shown as he healed the sick, forgave sins, and cast out demons, who represented the power of evil. People heard him gladly, but the leaders from Jerusalem, both Pharisees and Sadducees were concerned enough to investigate him. The former stood zealously for strict observance of the Law and thought he was too lenient and therefore irreligious; the latter favored rapprochement with the Roman authorities and thought that his appeal to the crowd would cause governmental reprisal.

Jesus taught the people, and sometimes taught his disciples privately, often using the parable as a form of illustrative story. Finally he decided that he must proclaim the kingdom in Jerusalem and do this when the greatest crowds were there for Passover. Gathering his disciples, he began the trip south. He asked who they thought he was, and Peter answered, "You are the Christ", i.e., the anointed one, but they were unprepared for his attempts to teach them that he must suffer and that his kingdom was not one of earthly power. Taking the inner three, Peter, James, and John, upon a mountain, he was transfigured before them, but instead of exciting in them a sense of mystery, this seems only to have stimulated their hopes for places of honor.

Jesus entered Jerusalem symbolically riding on a colt, acclaimed by pilgrims, many of whom would have known him from Galilee. He taught in the temple court, but prudently withdrew to nearby Bethany at night. When one of the disciples, Judas, agreed to betray him, the leaders were certain that he was finally in their power. Jesus stayed in the city one evening for a Passover supper with the Twelve, retired to the nearby Mount of Olives for a period of agonizing prayer at which the inner three were present, although sleeping, and was captured there. After trials through the night by both the Sanhedrin and the Roman courts, who alone could pass the death sentence, he was scourged and ordered crucified. This was carried out the next day and his body laid by friends in a borrowed tomb.

On the third day afterward, and for many succeeding days, his friends reported appearances among them: at the tomb, in the upper room, by the Sea of Galilee, and finally to a large group at a mountain where he announced that he would appear no more but would send his Spirit among them with power. With this assurance, companies of believers continued to meet and to affirm his continuing presence among them. (Matthew; Mark; Luke; John; Acts 1:1–11)

Jethro Jĕth'rō

Jethro was a priest of Midian (or of the Kenites) and the father-in-law of Moses, who had fled to this area when forced to leave Egypt. After Moses had returned to Egypt to secure the release of his people, his wife and two sons were sent back into Jethro's care. When the tribes had arrived in the Sinai area, Jethro brought Moses' wife and sons to him. He offered sacrifice and shared a ceremonial meal with the elders. The next day, observing that Moses spent most of his time hearing legal cases for the people, he advised that this unnecessarily wasted the leader's strength. He suggested the appointment of able men as judges, thus freeing Moses to handle only difficult situations and to teach the people. His plan was accepted. (Exod. 3:1; 4:18; 18:1–27)

Jezebel Jez′ė·bėl

Jezebel was a princess of Sidon and wife of King Ahab of Israel. She was a determined woman who used her power to gain her own ends. Brought up as a worshiper of Baal, she not only introduced this religion into her adopted country, but attempted also to erase the worship of Yahweh there by killing the prophets, who doubtless were vocally opposing her. This led to Elijah's challenge to the priests of Baal for the sacrifice on Mount Carmel. After the slaughter of the priests of Baal there, Jezebel sent word to Elijah that she would have him killed immediately, and he fled.

When Ahab desired Naboth's vineyard which lay beside the palace grounds, and Naboth refused to sell, Jezebel, believing that a king should have whatever he wanted, plotted the death of Naboth and gave possession of the land to her husband. This called forth the curse of Elijah, fulfilled many years later by Jehu. When the avenging usurper, who had already killed her husband, approached her house, she put on her makeup and presented herself proudly at the window. At Jehu's command, she was thrown to the ground and died. (I Kings 16:31; 18:1–18; 19:1–2; 21:5–15; II Kings 9:29–37)

Joab   Jō'ab

Joab was the commander of King David's army and probably the most influential person in his life. He may have been an early member of David's outlaw band. When David became acknowledged leader of Judah, Joab led the victory over Ishbaal, Saul's son and king of Israel. He murdered Ishbaal's commander, Abner, ostensibly in revenge for the death of Joab's brother in combat, a deed which David condemned but did not punish. Joab is credited with being the first to enter Jerusalem when the city was taken by David's men. During the successful campaign against the Ammonites he carried out David's message to put Uriah in the battlefront, with the result that Uriah was killed and David married his widow.

When Absalom was exiled for the murder of his stepbrother Ammon, his return was contrived through the influence of Joab. But when Absalom led a nearly successful revolt against the king, Joab led that wing of the army which found the young prince and, in spite of the king's orders, Joab killed him. When the king went into seclusion to mourn his son, Joab, with the familiarity of years, rebuked him for not rejoicing that the kingship was secured and told him that if he did not commend them for their loyalty, his men would forsake him. David accepted the advice, but replaced Joab as commander with Amasa. Joab faithfully followed in the campaign to subdue a rebellion by Sheba, a Benjaminite, but impatient with Amasa's delays, murdered him, took command, and subdued the revolt.

As the struggle for the succession developed in David's old age, Joab allied himself with Adonijah's party and when Soloman succeeded to the crown, Joab was killed, allegedly to avenge guilt for the murderers of Abner and Amasa. He had been David's most loyal and capable servant, enabling his friend and leader both to acquire and to keep the monarchy in spite of rebellion within and foes outside. (I Sam. 26:6; II Sam. 2:12–32; 3:24–30; 8:16; 20:23; 14; 18; 19:1–7, 13; 20; 24:3–9; I Kings 1:7; 2:28–34; I Chron. 2:16; 11:6)

Joanna   Jō·an′nà

Joanna was one of the women who were disciples of Jesus. Married to Chuza, a steward of King Herod Antipas, she was probably a woman of wealth and she contributed to the support of Jesus and his disciples. She is mentioned in Luke's Gospel as one of the women who went to his tomb with spices, received the message that he had risen, and returned to tell this to the unbelieving disciples. (Luke 8:3; 24:10)

Joash   Jō′ash *(see* **Jehoash***)*

Job   Jōb

Job, the leading character in the book bearing his name, was a good man upon whom disaster fell in the loss of his goods, the death of his children, and finally a painful disease. The background story says that God permitted Satan thus to tempt Job to see if his faith would endure. Job was visited by three friends who insisted that he must have sinned to have been so stricken, but Job defended himself. Finally Yahweh himself intervened and proclaimed that his ways are beyond human wisdom. Job submitted without further protest and health, goods, and family were restored to him. (Job)

Joel   Jō'ĕl

Joel is the name of a book by one of the prophets, but no information is given about the person. The book is a lament in the time of a plague of locusts and a call to repentance in the hope of God's deliverance. (Joel)

John   John

(1) John, called the baptizer, was the son of a priest, Zechariah, and his wife Elizabeth, in their older years. He was a cousin to Jesus. As a young man he made his appearance in the wilderness area of the Jordan River near the Dead Sea, dressed in animal skins and eating whatever he could forage. He had the appearance of a prophet and people asked if he were Elijah, forerunner of the Messiah, or even the Messiah himself, but he denied both appella-

tions. Warning people of the judgment of God, he preached repentance and offered them baptism upon confession of sins, exhorting them to a life of honesty. He announced the coming of the Messiah and interpreted his baptism as a preparation. Large crowds went into the wilderness to see and to hear him, for he was popular. Jesus came to him there and was baptized. This marked the beginning of Jesus' ministry, and it is thought by some that he did not begin his work until John's imprisonment. John denounced Herod Antipas for marrying Herodias, his brother's wife, and the king imprisoned him, hesitating to do violence because of John's reputation among the people. Becoming anxious in his solitude, John sent disciples to Jesus to ask if he were the Messiah. Jesus simply pointed to his work. Then to the people surrounding him he extolled John as a prophet and more: as in fact the messenger, Elijah. One day Salome, Herodias' daughter, danced before the king at a banquet and when he generously offered her any request, on her mother's advice she asked for the head of John the baptizer. The request was carried out forthwith. When Jesus heard of his death, he retired alone with his disciples. The disciples of John continued his witness and a group were found by Paul to be living in Ephesus. (Mark 1:4–14; 2:18ff.; 6:14–28; 9:13; Luke 7:18–35; John 1:19–36; 3:25ff.; Acts 18:25–19:3)

(2) John, son of the fisherman Zebedee and the brother of James, was one of the twelve disciples, indeed, one of the inner three, who shared in some experiences with Jesus from which the rest were excluded. He was present at the

healing of Peter's mother-in-law, the healing of Jairus' daughter, the transfiguration, a conversation about last things, and in Gethsemene just before Jesus' arrest. John and his brother James were named by Jesus "sons of thunder" (Boanerges), which suggests an explosive nature. When the company of disciples was refused entrance into a Samaritan village as they journeyed toward Jerusalem, John suggested that fire from heaven be called upon it. On one occasion he objected to the work of an exorcist who said he was a follower. The two brothers seem often to have acted together. Both asked for seats of honor in Jesus' kingdom, and were rebuked. Both were sent ahead of the rest to prepare the Passover meal. John and Peter seem to have worked together in the early days of the church at Jerusalem. He was with Peter when the latter healed a lame man at the temple gate and the two were arrested together, questioned, and later released. After the community had been dispersed, following the death of Stephen, John and Peter were sent to Samaria to a group of baptized believers for the laying on of hands that they might receive the Holy Spirit. They preached in other villages as they returned to Jerusalem. When Paul went to Jerusalem after his conversion he was received by John, who, Paul notes later, was a pillar of the church along with Peter and James.

John is not mentioned in the Gospel of John. He might have been the beloved disciple mentioned. The "unknown disciple" mentioned in that Gospel is still another person. It is usually assumed that the Gospel of John was not

written by the disciple but by one who became Christian
at a later time and lived in Asia Minor. That John is also
author of the three letters, and is there identified as John
the Elder. (Mark 1:19, 29; 3:17; 5:37; 9:2, 38; 10:35ff.;
13:3; 14:33; Acts 3:1–4:23; 8:14ff.; Gal. 2:9)

Jonah Jō'nàh

Jonah is the hero of the book which bears his name. The
prophet was called by God to go to Nineveh to warn that
the city would be destroyed if it did not repent. Evading
the call, Jonah sailed toward Tarshish, a storm arose, the
lot for the guilt fell on him, and he was thrown into the
sea. Swallowed by a great fish, he was regurgitated three
days later on dry land. Given a second chance, he went to
Nineveh and delivered the message. The people repented,
and Jonah, offended by the mercy shown by God, sulked
under the shade of a gourd. When the gourd withered,
Jonah was uncomfortable in the sun and wished himself
dead. God replied that if Jonah was so concerned about a
plant which he had not made, he should expect that God
would pity the people whom he had made. (Jonah)

Jonathan Jon'à·thàn

Jonathan, one of the sons of Saul, accompanied the army
in the struggles against the Philistines. On one occasion,
he and his armor-bearer surprised a garrison, killing twenty
men and caused such confusion that his father's army was
able to win a victory. Saul had ordered a fast that day,

with the death penalty to anyone who disobeyed. This was unknown to Jonathan, who, coming upon honey in the forest, dipped into it. When the sacred oracles consulted by Saul gave him no direction for the continuing battle, he sensed that something was wrong, and calling for lots, discovered that his son had broken the fast. He was determined that Jonathan should die, but the people refused to permit this and ransomed him.

As soon as Jonathan saw David, newly come into the king's service, he felt drawn to him and the two made a compact of friendship. When Saul's jealousy caused him to ask for David's death, Jonathan pleaded with his father and David was temporarily restored to favor. The next time David's life was in danger, Jonathan agreed to give a reason for his friend's absence from the king's table at a feast, thus sounding out his father's feelings. Saul's response was such anger at Jonathan's concern for David that he threw a spear in his son's direction. Jonathan, also angry, withdrew to give David an agreed-upon signal. He shot an arrow across a field and said to his servant seeking it, "The arrow is beyond you," which meant to David, "Danger: leave." The two friends embraced and parted. They met once again while David was an outlaw. Jonathan died with his father and brothers in the battle against the Philistines on Mount Gilboa. II Samuel 1 is David's moving lament for his friend and for his king. (I Sam. 14:1–45; 18:1–4; 19:1–7; 20; 23:16–18; 31)

Joram Jō'răm *(see **Jehoram***)

Joseph   Jō'sĕph

(1) Joseph was the eldest of two sons born to the patriarch Jacob by his favorite wife, Rachel. His mother died a few years later while giving birth to her second son. Joseph was one of the youngest sons in the family but his father's favorite, indicated by the gift of the long robe which signified luxury. He aroused the jealousy of his brothers by relating dreams in which everyone in the family bowed down before him, and by bringing critical reports of how they herded the flocks. Seeing him as a threat to their inheritance, the brothers contrived to destroy him one day when he was sent with provision to them as they worked a distance from the camp. He was at that time seventeen years old. Reuben persuaded them, instead of killing him, to put him into an empty pit. Later, when a caravan of slave traders came by, Judah suggested that he be sold.

Joseph was taken to Egypt where he became slave to Potiphar, an officer of the guard. Potiphar's wife attempted to seduce the young man, and, angered by his rebuff, she lied against him and caused his imprisonment. There he languished, interpreting dreams for other prisoners. Finally a former prisoner, restored to favor, remembered Joseph when Pharaoh was troubled by dreams. The young man interpreted the dreams to foretell seven years of prosperity followed by seven years of famine and urged that food be conserved accordingly. Pharaoh placed Joseph in charge of this work and gave him the daughter of a priest in marriage. Joseph was at that time thirty years old. When the famine came, it covered a wide area, and Jacob sent his sons to Egypt seeking to buy grain. They were recognized by Joseph, who bade them bring their younger brother when next they came. After that second trip, Joseph contrived to have a silver cup hidden in Benjamin's grainsack and then accused him of thievery. Noting the devotion with which the others protected their father's youngest son, Joseph concluded that the years had changed his brothers, and he revealed himself to them. After a joyful reunion, they returned home to report to their father. The whole family then resettled in the land of Goshen.

As the famine increased, people sold their cattle, then their land, and finally themselves into the service of Pharaoh. Joseph distributed seed grain on a crop-sharing basis and a feudal system was developed in Egypt. He lived to see his great-grandchildren. When he died his body was embalmed and buried in Egypt with the proviso that when his people finally returned to their own land, he would be interred in the family tomb at Shechem.

(2) Joseph, the husband of Mary, mother of Jesus, appears only in the infancy narratives. The coming of the child was revealed to him and Mary was given into his care. Danger to the child was also made known to him and he fled with them from Bethlehem to Egypt for safety. Joseph, although a resident of Nazareth, where he was a carpenter, belonged to the family of David and returned to Bethlehem to enroll in a census ordered by Caesar Augustus (*c.* 4 B.C.). After the family had returned to Nazareth, he must have taught his trade to Jesus, who is later referred

to as a carpenter. A devout man, he and Mary went annually to Jerusalem for the Passover. Taking the family to the Passover feast when Jesus was about twelve years old, he shared Mary's anxiety over the boy's disappearance, and went back to the city to find him. No mention is made of Joseph beyond this time and it is supposed that he died not many years later when the support of the family fell to the young carpenter, Jesus. (Matt. 1:18–25; 2:19–23; Luke 1:26–27; 2; Matt. 13:55)

Joshua Josh′u·à

Joshua appears early in the exodus narratives as an attendant of Moses and a military leader. He led an armed band against attacking Amalekites early in their travels and successfully repelled them. He accompanied Moses when the leader went up on Mount Sinai. He was one of the twelve men chosen to scout out the Promised Land, and with Caleb disputed the timid report of the majority and urged immediate entrance into Canaan. For this trust in God's leadership, it was promised that those two only of the generation then standing at the borders of the land would someday enter it.

A generation later, when Moses was close to death, he commissioned Joshua to be his successor to lead the people back into the land of Canaan. They crossed the Jordan River with ceremony. They conquered the cities of Jericho and Ai, and successfully defeated the various kings in the area. This was a cruel warfare lasting many years, but eventually the land was subdued and territory allotted to the various tribes for settlement. Joshua, now elderly, gathered the tribes together at Shechem to renew the covenant which God had made with their forefathers and with Moses, and to promise to serve him faithfully. So Joshua died and was buried in his tribal lands in Ephraim. (Exod. 17:8–14; 24:13; 32:17; 33:11; Num. 13:1–14:38; 27:12–23; Joshua)

Josiah Jō·sī′ăh

Josiah became king of Judah after the long reign of Manasseh, who had persecuted the prophets and encouraged idolatry, and the two-year reign of Ammon, his father, who was assassinated. Josiah was eight years old at his accession and from his youth was devoutly committed to serving God. While still a young man he ordered the destruction of altars to the Baals. Six years later work began on the repair of the temple. During construction, a book of the Law was discovered. The Law it contained is substantially the original material from the book of Deuteronomy. Josiah listened with care, then had the book read in the presence of the elders and of the people of Jerusalem. There he renewed the covenant and this was followed by a celebration of the Passover feast. Josiah reigned when the Assyrian empire was breaking up and Babylonian power was growing. Strengthening the religious life in Jerusalem was one way of uniting his people. During his reign he seems to have succeeded in regaining some of his nation's former lands, for it is recorded that he destroyed pagan shrines at Bethel and in the cities of Samaria. These moves aroused the fears of Egypt. Josiah challenged

Pharaoh Neco at the battle of Megiddo and was fatally wounded there. The prophet Jeremiah wrote of him that he ruled with justice and righteousness and was concerned for the poor. His reign was 640–609 B.C. (II Kings 21:23–23:30; II Chron. 34;35; Jer. 1:2ff.; 3:6; 22:15–16; Zeph. 1:1)

Jotham Jō′thăm

Jotham, son of Uzziah, began his reign in Judah as regent while his father was ill of leprosy. He was an upright king, as his father had been. He built a gate to the temple, the wall of Ophel, and cities in the hill country. He successfully fought against the Ammonites. There were invasions from Syria and from Israel. Jotham was twenty-five years old at the beginning of his reign, which lasted from 742 to 735 B.C. The prophets Isaiah, Hosea, and Micah were contemporaries. (II Kings 15:5; 32–36; II Chron. 27:1–9; Isa. 1:1; Hos. 1:1; Mic. 1:1)

Jubal Jü′băl (see **Tubal-cain**)

Judah Jü′dăh

Judah was one of the sons of Jacob by Leah. It is written of him that he showed compassion toward his young stepbrother Joseph when the brothers wished to kill him, and suggested that he be sold to slave traders. Years later, when the sons of Jacob had gone to Egypt for grain at a time of famine, the youngest son, Benjamin, was brought into Egypt at the command of the still unrecognized Joseph. Judah made himself responsible to Jacob for the safe return of this son, and when Benjamin's life was threatened, he offered his own as substitute. He married the daughter of Shua, a Canaanite, and was the father of Er, Onan and Shelah. (Gen. 29:35; 37:26ff.; 43:8ff.; 44:18–34)

Judas Iscariot   Jū′dàs Is·car′i·ŏt

Judas Iscariot was one of the twelve disciples of Jesus and is called "the traitor." The leaders who sought Jesus' death knew that because of his popularity, they would need to arrest him secretly, and they needed an informer to tell them where he would be. Judas agreed to betray him, and Jesus seems to have known this, because he remarked that someone who ate with him would betray him. Judas led the guard under cover of night to the Garden of Gethsemene and there indicated Jesus by a kiss. The Gospels give no reason for the betrayal, but it is recorded that after the payment of thirty silver pieces had been made, Judas returned it, went out, and hanged himself. (Mark 3:19; 14:10–11; 17–21; 43–52; Matt. 27:3–10)

Jude   Jūde

Jude is the name of one of the letters in the New Testament. Nothing is known of the writer. He may be one of those listed as belonging to the twelve disciples (also designated as Thaddaeus). He may be one noted as a brother of the Lord. (Mark 6:3; Luke 6:16; Acts 1:13; Jude)

Justus   Jŭs′tŭs *(see* **Crispus***)*

Laban   Lā′bàn

Laban was the brother of Rebekah and a kinsman of the house of Abraham. An Aramaean, he lived near Haran from where Abraham had come. When Jacob arrived at his tent as a fugitive, Laban received him. Agreeing to give his daughter Rachel in marriage in return for seven years' service, he substituted the veiled elder daughter, Leah, and justified this by the custom that the elder daughter must marry first. Rachel subsequently was given to Jacob, who served a total of twenty years and then asked to leave. Through his own trickery Jacob managed to increase his flocks beyond those of Laban's. Bitterness arose between the two households, Laban's sons fearing that the inheritance would go to Jacob as an adopted son. Jacob left in haste with his family and flocks and Laban pursued, protesting the theft of his daughters, who, according to Aramaean law, belonged to his family and not to the family of their husbands. An agreement was made whereby Jacob promised to treat his wives well, boundaries were established between the tribes, and Laban bade farewell to the family, and returned home. (Gen. 29:1–30; 30:25–31)

Lazarus   Laz′à·rùs

Lazarus, brother of Martha and Mary, was one of the disciples of Jesus, although not one of the Twelve. He lived in Bethany. The Gospels relate of him only the story of his being raised from death by Jesus. (John 11–12)

Leah Lē'ăh

Leah was the elder daughter of Laban and the first to be given in marriage to Jacob. She was never Jacob's favorite wife in spite of the fact that she bore him six sons and one daughter. Leah had to endure Rachel's constant envy, and always hoped in vain to feel honored by her husband as the mother of so many sons. (Gen. 29–30)

Lot Lot

Lot, grandson of Terah and nephew of Abraham, joined the family migration from Ur in Chaldea, first to Haran and then into Canaan. As the prosperity of the families increased, the land became too sparse to feed all the cattle; consequently tensions arose. Abraham gave Lot a choice of land as they separated and Lot chose to go east into the fertile Jordan valley. This proved dangerous when an alliance of valley kings captured Lot, who had settled at Sodom. When Abraham learned of his nephew's disaster he came to the rescue. Sodom's evil reputation led God to decide on its destruction; but at the plea of Abraham, Lot's family were spared and they fled the burning city to live in the hills. But Lot's wife, ignoring the warnings of angels, looked back as she fled the city and was turned into a pillar of salt. There his daughters, seeing themselves deprived of all hope of husbands, lay with their father after they had plied him with wine. From these unions

came the tribes of Moab and of Ammon. (Gen. 11:27ff.;
12:4ff.; 13:5–13; 14:12–16; 19:1–26, 30–38)

Luke   Lūke

Luke was a physician who accompanied the apostle Paul
in some of his work. He was with the apostle during his
imprisonment at Rome. Little is written about him but
there is a strong tradition which links him to the writing of
both Luke and Acts as works addressed to Gentile Christians. The "we" passage begins in Acts 20:5, where the
apostle is ending his third missionary journey and heading
toward Jerusalem, starting from Troas and making stops
all along the way to Caesarea and then Jerusalem. Luke
accompanied Paul, then a prisoner, on the stormy sea
voyage to Rome and, as references in letters indicate,
stayed near him at least during the two-year house arrest.
(Col. 4:14; II Tim. 4:11; Philem. 24; Rom. 16:21; possibly Acts 13:1)

Malachi   Mal'à·chī

Malachi is the name of the last book of the Old Testament
and means "my messenger." Nothing is known of the
writer. His brief book is an exhortation to learning the
teachings of the covenant, keeping these carefully, and
worshiping faithfully. (Malachi)

Manasseh Mà·nas′sèh

(1) Manasseh was the name of one of the two sons of Joseph, blessed by the grandfather Jacob but placed second to his younger brother, Ephraim. (Gen. 48)

(2) Manasseh was the son of the good king Hezekiah but the most evil of the kings of Judah. He was a vassal of the king of Assyria and his kingdom enjoyed peace during a long reign (687–642 B.C.). Anxious for Assyrian favor, he persecuted the worshipers of the God of Israel and encouraged the importation of idolatrous practices. He built altars even within the house of the Lord. He sacrificed his own son. He resorted to witchcraft. He persecuted the prophets and ordered the execution of many people. So intense was the campaign against the worshipers of God that the prophets declared God's intention to destroy Judah and Jerusalem because of Manasseh. A reaction set in after his death so that his son Amon was assassinated after a two-year reign and an eight-year-old grandson, Josiah, evidently educated by a devout remnant, came to the throne to restore the covenant religion of his people. (II Kings 21; II Chron. 33)

Mark Märk

Mark is assumed to be the writer of the Gospel which bears his name. His Jewish name was John, but he used also a Greek surname, and was referred to as John Mark. The earliest Christian community met at his mother's house in Jerusalem. He was related to Barnabas, who brought the young man with him when accompanying Paul to Antioch after a mission to Jerusalem. Becoming Barnabas' and Paul's assistant for a preaching journey, John Mark left them at Perga for a reason not disclosed in the records. When a second journey was planned, Paul refused to take him along; thus Barnabas and John Mark returned together to Cyprus. Later he must have been restored to favor, for he was with Paul in Rome after the apostle had been imprisoned. A reference in I Peter suggests the tradition that at one time John Mark was an interpreter for Peter. Hence it often has been surmised that the Gospel of Mark is based on Peter's remembrances of Jesus. (Acts 12:12; 16:37ff.; Col. 4:10; Philem. 24; I Pet. 5:13)

Martha   Mär′thà

Martha of Bethany, sister to Mary and Lazarus, was one of the friends of Jesus whose hospitality he enjoyed. Eager to please her guest through the meal she prepared, she is depicted in the Gospel story, in contrast to her sister Mary, cited as doing "one thing needful," that is, hearing the word. (Luke 10:38–42; John 11:1, 5)

Mary   Mâ′ry

(1) Mary the mother of Jesus, learned of his impending birth by angelic vision and her submission has made her the prototype of the obedient servant of God, as contrasted with Eve the disobedient. She accompanied Joseph to Bethlehem, where the child was born, went to the temple

at Jerusalem for the ceremonial rite of the infant's circumcision and her own rite of purification. Fleeing to Egypt from the wrath of Herod, she returned with Joseph and Jesus to Nazareth, where the child grew up. She accompanied her husband annually to the Passover feast at Jerusalem and the boy went with them in his twelfth year. Missing him after a day's journey homeward, she and Joseph returned to find him with the teachers in the temple. Mary may have been widowed when Jesus was a young man, for he seems to have assumed care over her and to have succeeded Joseph as the village carpenter. She was with her son at a marriage at Cana and returned with him to Capernaum, which fact suggests that when his ministry began she may have moved from Nazareth to the town which was his headquarters. It is said that once she accompanied her four sons to visit him, but when he was told of their presence, he replied that those who do God's will are his family. John's Gospel relates that Jesus, in the hour of his death, commended her to the care of the beloved disciple. Mary was present among the first Christian group who met in Jerusalem awaiting the gift of the Holy Spirit. (Matt. 1:18–2:23; Mark 3:31–35; 6:3; Luke 1:26–56; 2; John 2:1–5; 19:25–7; Acts 1:14)

(2) Mary of Magdala was one of the women who helped provide for Jesus and the Twelve by giving money. He had released her from the spell of demons and she probably was grateful for her healing. Mary was one of the faithful women present throughout the crucifixion of Jesus and she accompanied his body to the tomb. She went to

the tomb on the first day of the week to help anoint the body with spices, and received the message that he was not there. The risen Lord appeared to her there, for she had stayed on, thinking at first that the body had been removed. (Mark 16:1–8ff.; 15:40, 47; Luke 8:2; John 20:1–18)

(3) Mary, sister of Martha and Lazarus, lived in Bethany. Jesus visited their home and on one occasion commended Mary that her concern was to sit and listen to his words. John's Gospel relates that after the brother's death, Mary, hearing that Jesus had answered the message to come, left the house to meet him. During supper at their house, shortly before his death, Mary paid tribute to Jesus by pouring precious oil on his feet and wiping them with her hair. (Luke 10:39–42; John 11; 12:3–8)

Matthew   Mȧt′thew

Matthew was one of the twelve disciples. He was a tax collector for the Roman government, for which his own people would have despised him. When Jesus spoke to him, "Follow me," Matthew joined the company. He gave a feast at his house to which he invited his friends. This brought rebuke from the Pharisees as to the kind of acquaintances Jesus and his disciples kept. Jesus said that these were the people to whom he was sent. Matthew is usually identified with Levi, the tax collector named in two of the Gospels. Matthew may have made the collection of Jesus' sayings which were incorporated into the Gospel which bears his name. (Matt. 9:9–13; 10:3; Mark 2:13–17; Luke 5:27–32)

Matthias Mat·thī'ås

Matthias was the one chosen by lot to complete the circle of twelve disciples as replacement for Judas Iscariot. Nothing further is known about him. (Acts 1:23–36)

Melchizedek Mel·chiz'ê·dek

Melchizedek was the king of Salem (later Jerusalem) who blessed Abraham, and received gifts from him, after a military skirmish in which Abraham rescued some of his kinsmen from their foes. The name appears again in Ps. 110:4, "You are a priest for ever after the order of Melchizedek." Some scholars think the connection is that, as king of Salem, Melchizedek was also priest of El Elyon, the god of that city. Later, when Jerusalem became the holy city of Israel, the ancient association of Melchizedek and Abraham was seen as signifying the historical connections across the years between Israel and the city over which the priest-king Melchizedek once ruled. This same theme is picked up in a Christian context in Heb. 6–7. (Gen. 14:18–20)

Menahem Men'à·hem

Menahem was a usurper who became king of Israel by assassinating a previous usurper, Shallum. Shallum had reigned one month after assassinating King Zechariah, son of Jeroboam, who had reigned for only six months after his father's death. Menahem ruled for ten years, beginning in 745 B.C. He put down revolts with great cruelty and bought off Assyria by exacting money from his wealthy subjects. (II Kings 15:8–22)

Mephibosheth Me·phib′ō·sheth

Mephibosheth, a son of Jonathan, was brought into King David's household as an act of courtesy toward the family of King Saul, Jonathan's father. Mephibosheth was lame in both feet, having been dropped by a nurse in her haste to get away after the deaths of Saul and Jonathan. A servant of Saul named Ziba accused Mephibosheth of having sided with Absalom during his revolt against David, although Mephibosheth insisted that he had stayed in Jerusalem only because of his lameness and had asked Ziba to saddle a horse for him in order that he might follow the king. David, however, had already decided to divide Mephibosheth's land with Ziba. (II Sam. 9:1–13; 16:1–4; 19:25–31)

Meshach Mē′shack

Meshach was the Babylonian name given to Mishael, one of the three companions of Daniel. (Daniel)

Methuselah Mè·thü′sė·làh

Methuselah, son of Enoch, was the father of Lamech. He is said to have been 969 years old at his death and to have lived longer than any other person named in the Bible. (Gen. 5:21, 25–27)

Micah Mī′càh

Micah, whose name is given to one of the books of the prophets, came from the village of Moresheth, southwest of Jerusalem. He spoke during the reigns of Jotham, Ahaz, and Hezekiah (750–687 B.C.). He was a younger contemporary of Isaiah, and some of his emphases are similar to those of Isaiah. He lived at the end of the prosperous era in which Amos spoke, saw the invasion of Sennacherib, and knew his land as a vassal state. Like others of the prophets he insisted that he was no professional, but spoke because he felt the spirit of the Lord upon him. The book of Micah alternates threats against the nations with promises of restoration. He warns of the ultimate destruction of Jerusalem, a warning remembered later by Jeremiah (Jer. 26:18). Micah proclaims that this will be the judgment of God because of his people's idolatry, immorality, and injustice. (Micah)

Micaiah Mī·cāi′àh *(see* Jehosàhaphat*)*

Michal Mī′chàl *(see* David*)*

Miriam Mir′i·am

Miriam was the sister of Moses and Aaron. Born near the end of the Egyptian captivity of the Israelites, she may have been the daughter who saved the life of her infant brother Moses. Miriam, who is called a prophetess, probably was important as a leader during the Exodus. She led the women in triumphal song and dance after the Israelites had successfully escaped across the Reed (Red) Sea. Early in the journey Miriam, with Aaron, disputed the primary leadership of Moses, pressing their own position. When Miriam became leprous, this was interpreted as a sign of God's displeasure. However, the whole camp remained in that place during the period of Miriam's eight-day quarantine and cure. She died during the long stay at Kadesh-barnea, where the Israelites had encamped after hesitating to enter Canaan from the south. (Exod. 2:4–9; 15:20ff.; Num. 12:1–15; 21:1; 26:59; Mic. 6:4)

Mishael Mish′à·el *(see* **Meshach***)*

Mordecai Môr′de·cäi

Mordecai was the uncle of Esther, the Jewish girl who became queen to King Ahasuerus of Persia. He refused for religious reasons to give special honor to Haman, the king's chief agent. Haman then plotted to exterminate the Jews in the kingdom. With Esther's help, Mordecai was able to foil Haman's plot and was himself invested with Haman's former dignity and position. This story forms the background for the Jewish festival of Purim, and the book of Esther is read at that time. (Esther)

Moses Mō′s̄ēs

Moses was the most significant leader in the history of Israel, for he transformed the people into a nation yearning for one land and worshiping one God. Born during the height of his people's oppression in Egypt, he was saved from death in infancy because a princess adopted him. In young manhood, anger against a slave-driver caused him to murder the man and when he was taunted by one of his own people soon afterward, he fled in fear of detection. For years he lived with a Midianite tribe, marrying a wife there. In the experience of the burning bush, the name of the God of his forefathers was revealed to him, and he was told to demand the release of his people from slavery to return to Canaan, which they had left four hundred years earlier. Accompanied by his brother Aaron as a spokesman, Moses confronted Pharaoh many times, imploring and threatening. Finally, the plague which took the lives of the Egyptian firstborn sons convinced Pharaoh that the foreign slaves should be released. After successfully escaping across the Reed (Red) Sea, the Israelites made their way toward Mount Sinai, finding manna and quail to eat and water from a rock, all because of Moses' plea to God on their behalf. Their first military encounter was with the Amalekites. Moses' father-in-law, Jethro, visited, advising him on the distribution of responsibility so that Moses could be freed to give his time to the most important decisions.

Three months after leaving Egypt, the Israelites arrived at Sinai and Moses went up the mountain to worship in the presence of the Lord. He returned to punish the idolatry of the golden calf. Sinai is the setting for the giving of the Law and the building of the tabernacle to symbolize the presence of the Lord. Moses was the mediator through whom the covenant was made between Yahweh, their God, and the assembled tribes of Israel, in which they agreed to serve the Lord alone, faithfully and righteously, and the Lord promised to fulfill his purpose to make them a nation in their ancestral land of Canaan.

A census of the tribes was taken and in the second year after escaping from Egypt, the Israelites left Sinai. Scouts were sent into Canaan, but they reported back that the inhabitants were too strong to be conquered, and only two encouraged entry. An attempt to storm the hill country failed, and the tribes settled around the oasis at Kadesh-barnea for many years while the slave generation grew old and died and a free generation grew up. There were several revolts against Moses' leadership: by Miriam and Aaron, Jorah, Dathan, and Abiram. Repulsed when they attempted to enter Canaan through the Negeb, they circled east into Transjordan. They were denied entrance through Edom and reached Moab by an indirect route. Moses died in Moab, on the top of Mount Nebo, where he could view the Promised Land he would never enter. He left to his successor the task of crossing the Jordan River and the conquest of Canaan.

Moses did not command the army, did not officiate as priest, and delegated the administration of justice. He was the leader through whom his people developed a sense of identity, who persevered in the determination to return to Canaan, who forged the sense of covenantal relationship to God. (Exod. 1–20; 32–33; Num. 1:1–4; 10:11–36; Deut. 34)

Naaman   Nā′à·man

Naaman, commander of the Syrian army, was a leper. From an Israelite maid of his wife's he learned of the power of the prophet Elisha. The king of Syria received permission from the king of Israel for Naaman to visit Elisha. The prophet sent a message to him to wash in the Jordan River seven times, and by this action his leprosy would be cured. Rejoicing in his cure, he besought Elisha to accept a present. When Elisha refused, Naaman begged that he might be permitted to take some Israelite earth with him in order to be reminded of the Lord of Elisha. The incident points up the writer's desire to show the superiority of the God of Israel over foreign gods. (II Kings 5)

Nabal   Nā′bal *(see* **Abigail***)*

Naboth   Nā′bŏth

Naboth, a resident of Jezreel, owned a vineyard next to the palace of King Ahab, who wanted to purchase it for use as a vegetable garden. He refused to sell it, for it was a custom in Israel that land should be kept in a family which had owned it for a long time. Jezebel, Ahab's wife, noting her husband's displeasure over Naboth's refusal to sell, arranged to have Naboth charged with cursing God and the king, in punishment for which Naboth was stoned to death. Elijah announced to Ahab the Lord's curse against the royal family for this evil deed. (I Kings 21)

Nadab   Nā'dab *(see* **Baasha***)*

Naomi   Nā'o·mī

Naomi was the wife of Elimelech of Bethlehem and mother of two sons. During a famine, the family migrated to Moab, where in the course of time the sons married. When her husband and both the sons had died, Naomi decided to return to Bethlehem where she would still be remembered. One daughter-in-law, Ruth, accompanied her, and Naomi arranged that Ruth should harvest grain in the fields of a wealthy relative, Boaz, thus paving the way for Ruth's marriage to Boaz. (Ruth)

Nathan   Nā'than

Nathan was a prophet at the court of King David. He once told the king that he might build a temple, but later reversed this advice, promising him, rather, a continuing dynasty. He rebuked David for his adultery with Bathsheba and the murder of her husband and told him that the child would die. In David's old age, Nathan belonged to a group favoring Solomon as successor. He persuaded Bathsheba to ask this of the king, and then he also went to David in Solomon's behalf. Two of his sons were appointed officers in Solomon's court. Nathan was a court prophet, but exhibited the sense of justice associated with those prophets who considered themselves nonprofessional. While he would participate in court politics, he would also accuse a king. (II Sam. 7:1–17; 12:1–25; I Kings 1:8ff.; I Chron. 17:1–15)

Nathanael Nà·than'à·el

Nathanael was sought out by Philip after the latter had become a disciple of Jesus. On first hearing about Jesus from Philip, Nathanael had doubted, asking, "Can anything good come out of Nazareth?" But when he met Jesus he exclaimed, "Rabbi, you are the son of God! You are the King of Israel." His name does not appear in the lists of the Twelve, but it is thought that he is the same as Bartholomew or Matthias. (John 1:45–51; 21:1)

Nebuchadnezzar Ne·bù·chàd·nez'zàr

Nebuchadnezzar was actually Nebuchadnezzar II, king of Babylon (605–562 B.C.). He served as a general of his father's army, defeating Egypt at Carchemish, thus making it possible for Babylon to control the Syrian and Phoenician coasts. After succeeding his father he became a great builder, and his city of Babylon was considered a world-wonder. He fought against Judah and conquered Jerusalem in 598–597. This began the Babylonian exile, during which many Israelites, especially from the upper-class section of society, were exiled to Babylonia. (II Kings 24; Jer. 25–38; Ezek. 29–30)

Neco Nē'cō *(see Jehoiakim)*

Nehemiah Ne·hė·mī′åh

Nehemiah was a devout Jew living in Persia during the exile in the reign of King Artaxerxes, to whom he was a cupbearer. Hearing that an attempt to rebuild the walls of Jerusalem had been unsuccessful, he asked and received of the king permission to return to the city. He was appointed governor of Judea in 445 B.C. and held this office for twelve years. After his arrival in Jerusalem he inspected the walls at night and found true the reports that the fortifications were in ruins. Sanballat, governor of Samaria, who probably resented the rebuilding of Jerusalem as a political center, ridiculed him and found many ways of hindering the work. An armed guard stood beside the builders while construction continued. Citizens who were becoming indebted to unscrupulous lenders during this emergency complained, and Nehemiah insisted that no interest be exacted for loans, setting an example himself by lending money. Nehemiah refused a meeting with his opponents outside the walls, sensing a trap. Finally the walls were completed. Jerusalem needed more people, and lots were cast among citizens of nearby villages whereby one-tenth were removed to the city. A dedication of the walls was held, the covenant was renewed, and the people agreed to keep the Law more carefully; this included a promise to set aside their foreign marriages. Nehemiah went back to Persia. On a return visit to Jerusalem, however, he found that abuses had already crept in, including a continuation of the foreign marriages which he had denounced.

Again, the people promised faithfulness to the Law. (Nehemiah)

Nicodemus   Nic·ò·dē'mùs

Nicodemus, probably a member of the Sanhedrin, the chief judicial council of the Jews, came to see Jesus at night, wanting to have a conversation. He greeted Jesus as "a teacher come from God." There ensued the famous conversation about the need to be born anew to enter the kingdom of God. In a meeting of the Sanhedrin, when Jesus was being accused by the Pharisees, he spoke in defense of Jesus, by arguing, "Does our Law judge a man without first giving him a hearing and learning what he does?" After Jesus' death Nicodemus brought myrrh and aloes for the preparation of his body for burial. It is not certain whether he became a disciple. (John 3:1–15; 7:50; 19:39)

Noah   Nō'åh

Noah was a righteous man chosen to make the ship in which two of each species would be preserved during the great flood destroying an evil civilization. After the rain had ended and the waters receded, Noah and the others left the ark. He offered sacrifice to God, received a blessing and a promise that earth would never again be destroyed by flood. Noah was the first to cultivate the earth and to plant a vineyard. Once in harvest time he became drunk and was discovered naked by his son Ham, who ridiculed him. His other sons simply covered him. Awaking, Noah cursed Canaan, son of Ham. (Gen. 5:28–30; 6:11–9:28)

Obadiah Ō·bà·dī'ăh

Obadiah was a prophet whose name is borne by the shortest book in the Old Testament. No facts are known about him. His name means "servant of the Lord" and is used also as the name of a number of other minor characters in the Old Testament. The book of Obadiah is thought to have been produced some time after the fall of Jerusalem to Babylon in 587–586 B.C. The book contains a complaint against the Edomites for having been hostile when their neighbors were in peril, and predicts the coming of the "day of the Lord" and the return of the exiles to the Promised Land. (Obadiah)

Omri Om'rī

Omri was a king of Israel, 876–869 B.C. He had been commander of the army under Elah. Another officer, Zimri, assassinated Elah and made himself king, but the army proclaimed Omri king instead. Besieged at the city of Tirzah, Zimri burned the king's citadel while he himself was inside. The people were then divided between Omri and another leader, Tibni, but Omri won. During his reign he built the city of Samaria. The marriage of Omri's son Ahab to Jezebel led to an alliance with Tyre. His daughter Athaliah's marriage to Jehoram produced an alliance with Judah. Like Jeroboam, he permitted the worship of idols. (I Kings 16:16–29; II Chron. 22:2)

Onan   Ō'nån

Onan, second son of Judah, refused to have a child by Tamar, his brother Er's widow, to whom he had been given in marriage, because according to the Law such a child would have borne his brother's name instead of his own. This was considered sinful and was the cause of his death. (Gen. 38:4–10)

Onesimus   Ō·nes'i·mûs

Onesimus was the runaway slave about whom Paul's letter to Philemon was written. The name means "useful." He accompanied Tychicus to Colossae. (Philemon; Col. 4:9)

Ophni   Oph'nī

Ophni was a son of Eli, with whom he served as a priest at Shiloh. He and his brother Phinehas cohabited with temple prostitutes and extracted favors from people who had come to offer sacrifices. He and his brother were killed in a battle with the Philistines. (I Sam. 2; 4)

Paul   Päul

"Paul" was the Roman name taken by Saul. Born in Tarsus of Jewish parents, he was a citizen of both that city and Rome. He was a tentmaker by trade. As a young man he went to Jerusalem, shortly after the death of Jesus, to study the Law under the famous rabbi Gamaliel, and became a zealous Pharisee. This led him to participate in the stoning of Stephen and to become an agent of the Sanhedrin in pursuing Christians to Damascus. His vision of the risen Jesus speaking to him as he traveled toward Damascus turned his life around. After several days of blindness he was found by a disciple, Ananias, cured, and baptized. Saul retired to Arabia for three years, evidently unsure of his mission, then returned to Damascus where he preached to the Jews. He aroused their anger and had to leave the city secretly. He visited briefly with leaders of the church at Jerusalem, then returned to Tarsus for several years, evidently finding himself unacceptable to either Jews or Christians.

He was recalled to Antioch by Barnabas, through whom he became a teacher in the church there. The two carried an offering to the mother church at Jerusalem, then set out from Antioch on a preaching trip, mainly in Cyprus. This set the pattern for preaching first to the Jews, and only when rejected finding a way to preach to Gentiles. So successful was the mission to the Gentiles that he was called to Jerusalem, where the elders of the church worked out ground-rules for the admission of non-Jews. Paul seems to feel that he won his case.

The second preaching journey was made with Silas, after Paul and Barnabas had parted over the former's refusal to take along John Mark. This was the period during which he went into Europe, founding churches in Macedonia. During a two-year residence in Corinth, he founded the church there. On his third trip out of Antioch, he spent two years at Ephesus, starting the church there. Other trips had included harassment by Jewish groups; now, at Ephesus, a riot by silversmiths brought the first instance of Gentile persecution. Paul returned to Jerusalem, met with elders from the churches at both Ephesus and Miletus, and was warned that his life was in danger. He was carrying out purification rites in the temple when a riot began and he was arrested. Removed to Caesarea for safety, he spent some time imprisoned there. The governor, Felix, wanted a bribe, and his successor, Festus, professed to see nothing wrong in Paul's conduct, but carried out his appeal to Caesar. Paul was sent to Rome, shipwrecked on the way, and lived two years under house arrest. It is assumed that he was executed during an early persecution, before A.D. 68.

Paul was a man of determined opinions, fervent convictions, and strong feelings about people. Although he never knew Jesus, he is numbered among the apostles. He did not hesitate to challenge the opinions of the Jerusalem church, nor to assert his authority over churches of his own founding, such as that at Corinth. He was constantly troubled by what was probably an eye disease, and he endured persecution. His whole life revolved around his sense of being possessed by Christ, and although he speaks carefully of visions, he undoubtedly had mystical experiences. His brilliant mind explored the implications of Christian faith so definitively that Christian theology (both orthodox and heretical) has invariably had a start somewhere in his letters. He was the most important single person influencing the direction of Christian thought from its earliest days. (Acts; Letters of Paul. Note especially Acts 7:58; 9:1–30; 11:25–30; 13–28; autobiographical material in Rom. 11:1; I Cor. 15:8ff.; II Cor. 11:22–12:12; Gal. 1:11–2:14; Phil. 3:4–6; II Tim. 1:5; 3:10ff.)

Pekah   Pē′kảh

Pekah, an army captain under King Pekahiah, made himself king of Israel about 737 B.C. by assassinating his predecessor, who had reigned only two years. It was his hope to prevent conquest by the Assyrians, and to that end he joined an alliance with the king of Damascus to invade Judah and try to force its king, Ahaz, to join forces with them. The plan was unsuccessful. Tiglath-pileser and his Assyrian army made Israel a vassal state and were instrumental in the overthrow of Pekah by Hoshea. (II Kings 15:23–31; 16:5)

Peter Pē'tẻr

"Peter" is the descriptive surname given to Simon by Jesus. It means "rock" and suggests strength. With his father, Jonas, and brother, Andrew, he was a fisherman on the Sea of Galilee until early in Jesus' ministry when he was called to become a disciple. Peter came from Bethsaida but after his marriage lived in Capernaum. He is mentioned in the New Testament more often than any other of the disciples. Peter is the one who confessed Jesus as Messiah. He belonged to the inner circle of three disciples whom Jesus took along on special occasions: the raising of Jairus' daughter, the transfiguration, and the agony in the garden. He attempted to walk to Jesus across the water. He was sent with John to prepare the Last Supper, on which occasion he objected to having Jesus wash his feet. He wounded one of the men sent to capture Jesus, followed to the courtyard of the high priest where he three times denied knowing Jesus, and immediately left in deep remorse. He is always named first in the lists of disciples and of those who saw the risen Lord. Jesus commissioned him to leadership at the time of the confession at Caesarea Philippi and in the postresurrection world entrusted him with the responsibility of being shepherd.

Acts 1–12 shows him as a leader in the Jerusalem church, where he suggested the election of Judas' successor, preached to the crowds at Pentecost, healed a lame man, spoke before the council, was imprisoned and released. He was the first to carry the gospel to the Gentiles, receiving this call in a vision. On a later occasion, he refrained from eating with Gentiles, but nevertheless affirmed their right to baptism when Paul appeared before the council at Jerusalem.

There is a tradition linking him with the church at Rome, where it is said that he died in an early persecution. (Matt. 8:14; 14:28–31; Mark 1:16–20; 4:18–22; 5:37; 9:2; 10:2; 14:29–42; Luke 22:8; 24:34; John 13:6–9; 18:10; Acts 1–12; 15:7–11; I Cor. 9:5; Gal. 1:–18)

Philemon   Phi·le′mon

Philemon was a man of Colossae in Phrygia who had become a Christian under Paul's influence and in whose home the Christians met. While under arrest in Rome, Paul met Onesimus, a slave who had run away from Philemon's household and had been converted under Paul's influence. Under Roman law, Philemon had absolute authority over his slave. Paul writes in the letter to Philemon that he is returning Onesimus to him, urging that Philemon receive him back "no longer as a slave but more than a slave, as a beloved brother." (Philemon)

Philip   Phil′ip

(1) Philip was one of the twelve disciples. He came from the city of Bethsaida. When Jesus came to Galilee, Philip was invited to become a disciple. He in turn told Nathanael about Jesus and brought him also into the inner circle. Little is known about his life. He was present at the time the multitude were with Jesus, and expressed the opinion that even if they spent two hundred denarii

(about forty dollars) there would not be enough bread for each to get even a bit. He was approached by some Hellenistic Jews who had come to Jerusalem for the Passover and who wanted to meet Jesus. In one of Jesus' last conversations, Philip asked Jesus to show them the Father. Jesus' reply suggests that those who have seen him have seen the Father. (John 1:43–48; 6:5–7; 12:21–22; 14:8–9)

(2) Philip was one of the seven men chosen as deacons (assistants to the apostles) in Jerusalem. When a persecution arose against the church there, the disciples scattered, continuing to preach the gospel and to heal. Philip went to Samaria. There he converted many to the faith. One of his converts was Simon, a magician, who was baptized and stayed with Philip in his continuing work. While traveling on a desert road from Jerusalem to Gaza, Philip met an Ethiopian eunuch, the treasurer of Quee, Candace, who had been to Jerusalem for worship and was now reading Isaiah as he traveled in his chariot. Upon invitation, Philip joined him in the chariot and explained the passage. Philip related the prophet's word to Jesus, convincing the Ethiopian. When they came to some water, he asked Philip to baptize him. After that, Philip continued preaching along the coast in various towns until he came to Caesarea. He evidently settled in Caesarea, where he had four unmarried daughters who are said to have "prophesied." (Acts 6:5; 8:15–13; 8:26–40; 21:8–9)

Phinehas Phin′e·has *(see* **Eli***)*

Pilate Pī'late

In the creeds of the church, Pilate is mentioned as the person under whom Jesus "suffered." As procurator of Judea from A.D. 25 or 27 to 35, he was the Roman officer who sentenced Jesus to death. A few references to him in Josephus and Philip picture him as having been harsh against the Jews and the Samaritans. At one time he used money from the temple funds to build an aqueduct; when crowds gathered to protest, Pilate had many of them killed. At another time he had soldiers attack a Samaritan religious procession. When complaints about this action reached the ear of the legate of Syria, his superior, Pilate was sent to the emperor at Rome to explain his actions. When Jesus was brought before Pilate by the Jewish authorities, Pilate seems not to have considered him to have been proved guilty, even seeking to have Barabbas accepted as a substitute for execution. When the crowd insisted on Jesus' death, Pilate, before agreeing, washed his hands symbolically, saying, "I am innocent of this man's blood." Even though it was the Jewish custom for criminals' bodies to be thrown into a common grave, Pilate granted permission to Joseph of Arimathea to place Jesus' body in a new tomb. At the same time he granted permission to the Jewish authorities to have a guard of soldiers situated at the grave. (Matt. 27; Mark 15; Luke 23; John 18–19; Acts 3:13; 4:27; 13:28)

Potiphar Pot'i·phăr (see Joseph)

Rachel Rā′chel

Rachel was the younger daughter of Laban and a cousin to Jacob. Jacob loved her and served her father seven years to pay the bride price. When her sister was substituted, he worked another seven years for her. She bore no children for many years and gave her husband her slave, Bilhah, as a concubine. Finally she bore Joseph. When Jacob and his household returned to Canaan after twenty years, Rachel, in learning, stole her father's household gods—the symbol of family headship. Soon after the family had returned to Canaan, Rachel bore Benjamin and died in childbirth. (Gen. 29:6–31; 20:1–25; 31:14–35; 35:16–20; 48:7)

Rahab Rā′hab

Rahab was a prostitute whose house was built into the city wall of Jericho. She hid the two spies sent by Joshua to explore the city, denied their presence to the king, and sent them away secretly. They agreed that if she told no one of their business, they would spare her whole family if they were gathered together in her house when the city fell. The bargain was kept. Rahab and her family were taken into the camp of Israel before the burning of Jericho and lived among the Israelites thereafter. She is listed in Heb. 11 as one of the faithful. (Josh. 2:1–21; 6:17–25; Heb. 11:31)

Rebekah   Re·bek′ăh

Rebekah, daughter of Bethuel, became the wife of Isaac. Abraham had sent a trusted slave back to his family to seek a wife for his son. Tired at the end of the journey, he met at the well a young girl who offered water to him and his camels and at his request arranged lodging at her father's house. This was a sign to the slave. He made known his mission to the girl's father and brother, who accepted the proposal. The next morning Rebekah chose to go immediately to her new home, forgoing ten days of preparation in her parents' house. She became Isaac's wife and he loved her. She bore him twin sons: Esau and Jacob. Rebekah seems to have favored the latter, for she helped Jacob trick his elderly father into giving him the blessing intended for the firstborn, Esau. Then she arranged for him to escape his brother's wrath by returning to her family to find a wife. At her death she was buried at Machpelah with the other patriarchs and their wives. (Gen. 24; 25:23; 26:6–11; 27:1–28:5; 49:31)

Rehoboam   Rē·hȯ·bō′ăm

Rehoboam, son of Solomon, succeeded his father as king, reigning from 922 to 915 B.C. At this time it was still required that a king be approved by the assembly of the tribes. Representatives of the northern tribes complained about the late Solomon's severity. At Shechem, where he was to be made king, Rehoboam told Jeroboam and others from the northern region that he would be a sterner taskmaster than his father had been. This angered the northerners, who refused to give their allegiance to Rehoboam and set up the separate kingdom of Israel. Rehoboam was dissuaded from fighting against the northern tribes by the prophet Shemaiah. In his reign the palace and the temple were plundered during an attack by the Egyptian king Shishak. He built a number of fortified cities. (I Kings 12; 14; II Chron. 10–12)

Reuben   Reü'ben

Reuben was the oldest son of Jacob and Leah, and the oldest of Jacob's twelve sons. At one time in his youth, he had intercourse with Bilhah, one of his father's concubines, but although Jacob heard of this, he ignored it. As the elder son, Reuben evidently had influence among his brothers. When they wanted to kill Joseph, he persuaded them to throw him into the pit instead. Later, when the brothers went to Egypt seeking grain during a famine in their own land, they began to feel guilty because they had sold Joseph into slavery. Reuben reminded them that he had warned them not to harm the youth, suggesting that the time of reckoning had now come. When Joseph demanded that Benjamin be brought to Egypt, Jacob resisted, but was persuaded in part by Reuben's offer to leave his own sons with Jacob as a surety for Benjamin's safe return. (Gen. 29:32; 35:22; 37:21–24, 29–30; 42:22, 37)

Ruth Ruth

Ruth, a Moabite woman, married the son of Elimelech of Bethlehem and his wife Naomi, who had gone to Moab during a famine in their own country. After Elimelech and their two sons died, Naomi decided to return to Bethlehem. Ruth returned with her. In search of food, Ruth went to the fields of Boaz, a relative of Naomi's, to gather grain. Boaz noticed her and told his men to give her extra grain. Ruth told her mother-in-law about Boaz's generosity and Naomi suggested that Ruth return to Boaz and offer herself to him as his wife. Boaz desired her but first had to get permission from an even closer relative who would have had first claim on her. They were married, and their son Obed became the ancestor of David. The book of Ruth is written in such a way as to develop sympathy for Ruth, a foreigner, who chose to put herself under the God of the Israelites. (Ruth)

Salome Sa·lō′mē

(1) Salome was the daughter of Philip and Herodias. When a young girl, she danced before the guests at a banquet given in celebration of the birthday of King Herod Antipas, her mother's husband. Pleased, Herod

promised to give her whatever she might ask, and, at her mother's prompting, she requested the head of John the Baptist on a platter. (Matt. 14:1–12; Mark 6:17–29)

(2) Salome was the wife of Zebedee and mother of James and John, the apostles. She once asked Jesus to give her sons favored places in his kingdom. She was one of those who stood by Jesus, in the background, during his crucifixion. With the Marys, she went to the tomb and heard the announcement of the resurrection. (Matt. 20:20–28; Mark 15:40–41; 16:1)

Samson Săm'sŏn

Samson, son of Manoah, was born in Zorah. The announcement of his coming birth is set in the form of an angelic message to the mother, predicting that her child would be devoted as a Nazirite to God and that he would deliver Israel from the Philistines. The boy was raised austerely, never having his hair cut, avoiding wine, and keeping the dietary laws strictly. At Timnah he fell in love with a Philistine woman whom he married; but because she revealed to her own people the answer to a riddle he told at the wedding feast, the marriage was soon ended. Samson is depicted as a man of tremendous strength and bravado, the hero of wild and amazing exploits. Betrayed by Delilah, a Philistine mistress to whom he entrusted the secret of his strength, that a razor had never touched his head, his hair was cut off while he slept. Weakened by the loss of his hair, he was seized by Philistines who gouged out his eyes and bound him in bronze chains. When his hair grew out, his strength returned. One day his captors, seeking to make sport of him, arranged a feast to their god Dagon and led the blind Samson to a house where people were assembled in large numbers. Assisted in reaching for the pillars of the porch, he was able through his great strength to cause the building to collapse. Samson and all the Philistines inside were killed. He was included among the judges of Israel, having served in that capacity for twenty years. (Judg. 13–16)

Samuel Săm′ū·el

Samuel was born to Elkanah by Hannah, who had yearned for a child without avail. Hannah's prayer was granted and the first son she bore was dedicated to God. The boy was placed in the care of Eli, the priest at Shiloh, who had two dissolute sons, Ophni and Phinehas. Young Samuel, who assisted Eli the priest, received a message from the Lord that the sons of Eli would be destroyed because of their sins. They were later killed in a battle with the Philistines. In that same battle the ark itself was captured by the enemy, who returned it because they were troubled with the plague after its capture. Samuel emerged as the leader of a confederacy of the tribes. When the people demanded a king, Samuel at first opposed the idea. Eventually he selected Saul to be the king of Israel. Having anointed Saul as king, Samuel continued in a leadership role, even to the extent of reprimanding the king. Finally he told Saul that because he had not destroyed the king of the Amalekites as commanded, he must be deprived of the kingship. Samuel then went to Bethlehem to anoint David as Saul's successor. Samuel was the last of the judges, a king-maker and a power behind the throne. When he died, he was buried at Ramah. (I Sam. 1–25)

Sanballat   San·bal'lât *(see* **Nehemiah***)*

Sapphira   Sap·phī'râ

Sapphira was the wife of Ananias. Both were members of the early church at Jerusalem. Together they kept back from the church a part of their profits from the sale of land. When Peter accused them of lying, each, being confronted by him separately, died instantly. (Acts. 5:1–11)

Sarah   Sâr'äi

Sarah was the wife of the patriarch Abraham. Having no children, she gave her slave Hagar to Abraham but later resented Hagar and had her thrown out of the household. In her old age she conceived and bore a son, Isaac. On two occasions Abraham said that she was his sister and she was received into harems of other men: a Pharaoh and a king of Gerar named Abimelech. When she died at Hebron, she was buried in the cave of Machpelah. The people of Israel were always reminded of Abraham and Sarah, as in Isa. 51:2: "Hearken to me, you who pursue deliverance, you who seek the Lord; look to the rock from which you were digged. Look to Abraham your father and to Sarah who bore you." (Gen. 11–23)

Saul Saul

(1) Saul was a tall handsome man, the son of a wealthy Benjaminite. When the people of Israel demanded a king, Samuel anointed Saul. He was chosen by lot at a gathering of the tribes at Mizpah and proclaimed king before all the people. His first successful battle was against Jabesh. He carried out a long campaign against the Philistines, during which his son Jonathan nearly became a sacrifice for having unwittingly ignored Saul's order that the army fast. Young David's combat with the Philistine champion Goliath introduced David into the court. Saul promised David his elder daughter for a wife, but gave her to another man. He then offered his younger daughter on the condition that David kill a hundred Philistines. David succeeded and so evaded this attempt by the king first to cause his death.

Meanwhile Saul had aroused the anger of Samuel, who did not approve of kingship. First Saul performed a sacrifice without awaiting Samuel's tardy arrival (there was no official priesthood at that time). Next he disobeyed Samuel's order from the Lord after the defeat of the Amalekites and spared both their king and the choicest spoils. Samuel denounced and rejected the king to his face. This seems to have begun a mental breakdown which was augmented by the rising popularity of David. David had come into the king's household to soothe his angers and depressions with music, but Saul became obsessively jealous. Twice he tried to kill the young man in the house, and once he threw a spear at Jonathan for defending him. When David, aided by his wife Michal and by Jonathan, fled, the king ignored other responsibilities to chase him throughout the land. He murdered the priests of Nob who had befriended David. Twice David reached the king's tent but spared him. Now the Philistines began to attack. Saul, in desperation, feeling forsaken by the Lord, consulted a medium at Endor to summon the ghost of Samuel, who affirmed that Saul would die and his kingdom belong to David. Saul met the Philistine army on Mount Gilboa, and, badly wounded, killed himself. His three sons died with him there. His loyal men obtained the bodies and gave them burial. He reigned from about 1020 to 1000 B.C. David's lament over his king, in II Sam. 1 is authentic and moving. Saul had been a leader in Israel and his work made possible the monarchy which was to follow. (I Sam. 9–11; 13–15; 17–24; 26–28; 31; II Sam. 1:19–27)

(2) Saul was the original name of the apostle Paul. (*see also* **Paul**)

Sennacherib   Sen·nach′ĕ·rib

Sennacherib was king of Assyria from 705 to 681 B.C. Faced with rebellions by subject peoples, including Syria and Palestine, he moved in 701 against Hezekiah, leader of the rebellion in Judah, and took Jerusalem. (II Kings 18–19; Isa. 36–37)

Sergius Paulus   Sĕr′gi·ŭs Päul′ŭs

Sergius Paulus, proconsul of Cyprus, asked Paul and Barnabas to talk to him about the Christian gospel. A magician named Bar-Jesus (also called Elymas) who was with Sergius Paulus tried to divert his attention from their claims for the gospel. Paul turned to the magician and called him "son of the devil, enemy of all righteousness, full of all deceit and villainy." Shocked by this accusation, the magician became blind, and Sergius Paulus believed in the gospel. (Acts 13:4–12)

Seth   Sèth

Seth was a son born to Adam and Eve after the death of Abel at the hands of his brother Cain. Seth had a son named Enosh. (Gen. 4:25–26)

Shadrach   Shā'drăch

Shadrach was one of the four young men brought into the household of Nebuchadnezzar to study the language and letters of the Chaldeans. His Israelite name had been Hananiah. He and the others refused to bow before Nebuchadnezzar's statue, and were thrown into a fiery furnace. As a reward for their faithfulness they were saved. (Daniel)

Sheba, Queen of   Shē'bà

Having heard about the wisdom and piety of King Solomon, the Queen of Sheba, a country on the Arabian peninsula in the region known today as Yemen, decided to visit King Solomon in Jerusalem. She brought a great caravan of camels, bearing gifts of spices, gold, and precious stones. She also brought many questions about which she wished to converse with Solomon. She was impressed with his ability to talk about these matters of interest to her. She was also impressed by the magnificence of the royal court which he had established. She was so delighted with all that she found in Solomon's realm that she exclaimed, "Because the Lord loved Israel for ever, he has made you king, that you may execute justice and righteousness." In departing, the queen accepted many presents offered her by Solomon in honor of her visit. (I Kings 10:1–13)

Shelah   Shē′làh *(see* **Tamar, 1***)*

Shem   Shèm

Shem was a son of Noah, brother of Ham and Japheth. He and his brother Japheth found their father lying naked after a bout of heavy drinking. They thoughtfully covered his body while he slept. When Noah awoke he was so pleased with their action that he gave them a special blessing.

Shemaiah   She·māi′àh *(see* **Rehoboam***)*

Shishak   Shī′shak *(see* **Rehoboam***)*

Shua   Shü′à *(see* **Judah***)*

Silas   Sī′las

When the Jerusalem council reached decisions concerning Gentile Christians, it was decided to send representatives to the church at Antioch to inform them of their conclusions. Among these was Silas, a Jerusalem Christian. Silas also went with Paul on his second missionary journey, sharing in the imprisonment at Philippi and the riot at Thessalonica. (Acts 15:22–25, 36–41; 16:1–11; 17:1–9)

Simon Sī·mòn

(1) Simon was the given name of the apostle Peter. (*see also* **Peter**)

(2) Simon the Zealot was one of the twelve disciples. The Zealots were Jewish patriots who were willing to use insurrection in the hope of freeing their people from Roman rule. (Matt. 10:4; Mark 3:18; Luke 6:15; Acts 1:13)

(3) Simon of Cyrene was among the onlookers when Jesus was carrying his cross to Golgotha. Seeing the fatigue of the prisoner, the soldiers pressed Simon into service and made him bear the cross. Two of his sons, Alexander and Rufus, were members of the early Christian community. (Mark 15:21)

Sisera Sis′ẻr·à *(see* **Barak***)*

Solomon Sòl′o·mon

Solomon, the son of King David and Bathsheba, was king of Israel from about 961 to 922 B.C. His given name was Jedidiah, and "Solomon" (meaning "peace," "prosperity") was probably a throne name, taken at his accession. Although Adonijah was the oldest living son, Solomon was the son of the favorite wife, and through court politics was named co-regent by David in his old age. Solomon, immediately after his accession, ordered the death of his opponents, especially any possible claimants to the throne.

Solomon's reign was long and peaceful. He extended the borders of the land, engaged in broad public works, built a temple and magnificent palaces, established store cities where chariots and horses were kept, developed mines, and traded in gold with countries on the Red Sea. All this involved heavy taxation and eventually the forced labor of his subjects. Solomon divided the kingdom into twelve districts, not entirely along tribal lines, thus weakening those older loyalties. His power enabled him to maintain a large harem, many of his wives including an Egyptian princess, representing alliances with neighboring states. His wealth became a byword and was mentioned even in New Testament times, but he so overspent that at one time he had to cede twenty cities to King Hiram of Tyre in payment for materials.

Solomon had a reputation for wisdom, and this may reflect the development of written literature—historical annals, psalms, and wisdom writings—during his reign. Although his greatness was extolled in the Chronicles, his intensive taxing and spending must have weakened the nation, since it fell apart soon after his death. (I Kings 1–11; II Chron. 1–9)

Stephen Stē′phen

Stephen was a Jew, born in the Diaspora, who became a Christian. Dissension developed early between the Pales-

tinian and the Diaspora Jewish Christians. This first took
the form of complaints of neglect in food distribution.
The apostles appointed six deacons to take care of this
service, and Stephen was one of them. His miraculous signs
and potent preaching aroused anger among Diaspora Jews,
who accused him to the council of speaking against the
temple and the Law. His defense is a summary of God's
saving work in Israel and the proclamation of the good
news in Jesus. The angry crowd would not permit him to
finish but rushed him off and stoned him. Stephen is
regarded as the first Christian martyr. (Acts 6–8)

Tamar Tā′mär

(1) Tamar was the wife of Er, the firstborn son of
Judah. When Er died, Judah gave her in marriage to his
second son, Onan, who also died. Fearing that his third
son, Shelah, might also die if he was promised to Tamar as
a husband, Judah told Tamar to return to her father's
household and remain there as a widow until Shelah grew
up. Years later, after the death of Judah's wife, the daughter of the Caananite Shua, Judah went to the region of
Tamar's father on business connected with his sheep. Hearing that he was in the area, Tamar dressed as a harlot and
sat at the village entrance. Judah, not knowing that she
was his daughter-in-law, had sexual intercourse with her,

during which she conceived. She had arranged this to spite Judah, "for she saw that Shelah was grown up, and she had not been given to him in marriage." She gave birth to twins by Judah, named Perez and Zerah. (Gen. 38)

(2) Tamar, a daughter of David, sister of Absalom, is described as "beautiful." David's son, Amnon, half-brother to Tamar and Absalom, fell in love with her. He seduced her into his tent, feigning sickness, and had intercourse with her. Instead of asking permission to marry Tamar, as she pleaded, Amnon refused to have anything further to do with her. Tamar went about the streets publicly acknowledging that her virginity had been violated by her half-brother. Absalom sought to comfort his sister and secretly planned eventual revenge. After two years Absalom killed Amnon at a sheep-shearing feast to which all his brothers had been invited. (II Sam. 13)

Terah Tē'ràh

Terah, son of Nahor, ·was the father of Abraham. A native of Ur, he intended to migrate with his family to Canaan; he stopped however, in Haran and settled there instead. He is said to have lived 205˙ years. (Gen. 11:24–32)

Thaddaeus Thàd·dae͞'ŭs

Thaddaeus, one of the twelve disciples, is completely unknown except for the listing of his name. (Matt. 10:3; Mark 3:18)

Theophilus   Thē·oph′i·lŭs

Luke's Gospel and Acts are dedicated to Theophilus, who in the Gospel is called "most excellent." The name means "beloved of God." (Luke 1:3; Acts 1:1)

Thomas   Thŏm′as

Thomas was one of the twelve disciples. He is called "the twin." Associated with his name are several well-known incidents and sayings. He asked Jesus, "Lord, we do not know where you are going; how can we know the way?" Not having been present at the first appearance of Jesus in the resurrection, Thomas expressed doubt: "Unless I see in his hands the print of the nails, and place my finger in the mark of the nails, and place my hand in his side, I will not believe." Later, seeing the risen Christ, he exclaimed, "My Lord and my God." (Matt. 10:3; Mark 3:18; Luke 6:15; John 11:16; 14:5; 20:24–29)

Tiberius   Tī·bē′ri·ŭs

Tiberius (Tiberius Claudius Nero), an adopted son, and stepson, of Augustus, was Roman emperor A.D. 14–37, succeeding his father. He was born in 42 B.C. His mother, Livia, had divorced Tiberius' father. John the Baptist's ministry began in the fifteenth year of Tiberius' reign. (Luke 3:1–3)

Tibni   Tib′nī *(see* **Omri***)*

Tilgath-pileser   Til'gath-pil·nē'sėr

Tilgath-pileser (also spelled Tiglath-pilneser), is considered to have been the founder of the Assyrian empire. He gained power in a country that had lost prestige and influence. He conquered Babylon and became its king also, attempting to fuse the Assyrian and Babylonian monarchies. In 734 B.C. he conquered Galilee and Gilead, and in 732 Damascus, and made them Assyrian provinces. King Ahaz of Judah sought Tilgath-pileser's aid against the kings of Israel and Syria, but he failed to profit even temporarily in spite of paying tribute to Tilgath-pileser. (II Chron. 28:20)

Timothy   Tim'ȯ·thy

Timothy was a follower and traveling companion of Paul's. He was a native of Lystra. His mother, Eunice, was a Jewish Christian and his father was a Greek. He had been circumcised as a Jew. His grandmother Lois had been a member of one of the earliest Christian families. It was during Paul's second missionary journey that Timothy was chosen to accompany the apostle, setting out with him from Lystra. At Berea Paul was forced to leave suddenly because of opposition from Thessalonian Jews. Timothy and Silas, another companion of Paul's, remained there, and eventually they were all able to rejoin one another at Corinth. Timothy went on some "trouble-shooting" journeys for Paul, such as to Macedonia (with Erastus), Thessalonica, and Corinth. At one point he was imprisoned and released. The letters I and II Timothy are addressed to him. (Acts 19:22; I Thess. 3:2,6; Heb. 13:23; I and II Tim.)

Titus Tī'tus

Titus, whose parents were Gentiles, went with Paul, Barnabas, and other Christians from Antioch to Jerusalem for the apostolic council. He also had gone to Corinth at Paul's request to ascertain the reaction of the church there to a letter, not now extant, that Paul had written "out of much affliction and anguish of heart and with many tears." Unwilling to wait for Titus' return, Paul left Ephesus, failing to meet him in Troas but doing so in Macedonia. There Titus brought word that the Corinthians still regarded him with affection. He also went to Crete and Dalmatia to organize churches. (Acts 15:2; Gal. 2:1–3; II Cor. 2:4; II Tim. 4:10)

Trophimus Troph'i·mùs

Trophimus, a Christian from Ephesus, was among those who went with Paul to Jerusalem. When Paul was accused of having brought Greeks into the temple, it was because he had been seen in the company of Trophimus. The only other fact we have about Trophimus is that he had to interrupt his participation in a journey when he became ill at Miletus. (Acts 20:4; 21:29; II Tim. 4:20)

Tubal-cain Tü'bàl-cāin

Tubal-cain was the son of Lamech and Zillah. He is regarded as the first to forge instruments of bronze and iron. He had a sister named Naamah and two half-brothers, Jabal and Jubal. (Gen. 4:19–22)

Tychicus   Tych′i·cùs

Tychicus, called an "Asian," probably came from Ephesus. He went with Paul and others on the journey to Jerusalem. He seems to have carried Paul's greetings and news to the Ephesians as a "beloved brother and faithful minister in the Lord." The name may be derived from that of the goddess Tyche, meaning "fortune". (Acts 20:4; Eph. 6:21)

Uriah   U·rī′åh

Uriah is mentioned among the thirty mighty, or chief, men of David's military entourage. Known as Uriah the Hittite, he was away in battle when David fell in love with his wife, Bathsheba, who became pregnant by David. To protect her and himself, David sent for Uriah in the guise of asking how the war was progressing. His real intention was to get Uriah to sleep with Bathsheba, but Uriah refused to do so, even after having been regaled with food and drink. David then sent word to Joab that Uriah should be put into the front fighting lines in order to make sure that he would be slain. That was done. In I Kings 15:5

David's arranging for Uriah's death at the hands of the enemy is referred to as the only time in which David did not do what was right in the sight of the Lord. (II Sam. 11; 23:29; I Chron. 1:41.)

Uzziah Uz·zī'ah

Uzziah (also known as Azariah), successor to Amaziah as king of Judah, was only sixteen when he became king, and ruled about half a century, 783–742 B.C. His reign was marked by peace, prosperity, and friendly relations with King Jeroboam II of Israel. The only complaint against him is listed as his having still allowed the people to worship at pagan shrines. He was stricken with leprosy, having to live apart from the palace while his son Jothan served as regent. The ministry of the prophet Isaiah began in the last year of his reign. (II Kings 14:21ff.; 15:17; II Chron. 26)

Vashti Vash'tī *(see* **Ahasuerus***)*

Zacchaeus   Zac·chae′us

Zacchaeus, the chief tax collector of Jericho, had become rich through extorting money from the poor. He was attracted into the crowd of people who gathered when Jesus passed through his city. Since he was short in height, he could not see Jesus from behind the crowd. He climbed into a sycamore tree. Jesus noticed him in the branches, called him down, and said that he would like to visit at his house, to which they went. Evidently moved by Jesus, Zacchaeus confessed his extortions and vowed that he would give half his goods to the poor, restoring fourfold anything that he had taken unlawfully. Jesus assured Zacchaeus that from that time "salvation has come to this house." (Luke 19:1–10)

Zadok   Zā′dok

Zadok was a priest appointed by David. He was one of the priests who followed David with the ark when, at the beginning of Absalom's rebellion, David left the city. David instructed the priests to return with the ark to Jerusalem, from which they kept David informed about Absalom's plans. Zadok remained faithful to David while his brother priest, Abiathar, supported Adonijah, David's oldest living son, for the kingship. When Solomon rather than Adonijah was chosen as David's successor, David ordered Zadok to anoint Solomon as king. In Ezekiel's restored temple the sons of Zadok were named as those who were to serve as priests. (II Sam. 15:24–35; 17:15; 18:19–27; Ezek. 44:15)

Zechariah   Zech·a·rī′åh

(1) Zechariah was a prophet (520–518 B.C.) whose ideas are contained in chapters 1–8 of the book of Zechariah. He was a contemporary of Haggai and encouraged the rebuilding of the temple. He argued that the people should repent and be purified in light of the coming of the messianic age. He wrote of visions that he had in the night-time.

(2) Zechariah was a priest during the reign of Herod the Great. He and his wife Elizabeth had not had children. One day as he was burning incense in the temple, the angel Gabriel appeared before the altar and announced that they would have a son, who was to be named John. He is said to have been struck dumb by the vision. After their baby was born, Elizabeth said at his circumcision that his name would be John. Relatives protested that no one in their family had been named that, and turned to Zechariah for a decision. Since he was still without speech, he wrote on a tablet, "His name is John." At that point his lips were opened and he gave praise to God. His words are preserved in the hymn called *Benedictus*. The child grew up to become John the Baptist. The name Zechariah means "Yahweh has remembered." (Luke 1:5–80)

Zedekiah   Zed·è·kī′àh

Zedekiah, the last king of Judah, a son of Josiah, reigned 597–587 B.C. Originally named Mattaniah, he was set up as a puppet king under the name Zedekiah by Nebuchadnezzar, king of Babylon, who controlled Judah. Zedekiah joined with other subject kings in an effort to instigate an insurrection. The prophet Jeremiah denounced this move, predicting that it would not succeed and urging Zedekiah to put his trust in God alone. Zedekiah seems to have wanted to listen to Jeremiah, but heeded his palace advisers instead. At once armies were sent by the Babylonians, which overran Judah and finally destroyed Jerusalem in July 586. Zedekiah was captured and taken to Nebuchadnezzar at Riblah. There he was put into chains, his sons were executed before his eyes, and he himself was blinded and carried away into exile in Babylon. Nothing more is known about him; presumably he died in exile. (Jer. 24; 52)

Zephaniah   Zeph·à·nī′àh

Zephaniah was a prophet who flourished about 630 B.C., before the famous reforms which Josiah effected in 621. He wrote portions of the book which bears his name. In it judgments are pronounced against Israel and foreign nations and a "day of Yahweh" is heralded. He is referred to as a descendant of Hezekiah, but it is not thought likely that his forebear was the king of Judah by that name. (Zephaniah)

Zerubbabel   Ze·rub'bà·bel

Zerubbabel, a descendant of David, was appointed governor of Judah during the period after the Babylonian exile, while the temple was being rebuilt. It is possible that he had led one of the first groups of Jews back to Jerusalem from Babylon. He and the high priest Joshua began the work on rebuilding the temple. Although the prophet Haggai apparently felt that Zerubbabel would be the bright future leader of the people, perhaps sometime even king of Judah, such a prophecy was never to be fulfilled. He vanishes from the story. Perhaps Persia was suspicious of a descendant of David's getting so much support from the people as to make him a threat to their power. No one knows whether he was removed from power or executed. (Hag. 1:12–15; 2:20–23)